*D*avid Carpenter is the author of several books of fiction including *Jewels*, *Jokes for the Apocalypse*, and *God's Bedfellows*, all of which have been praised by critics and readers for their wit and artistry. He co-wrote and edited *Fishing in the West*, a how-to book on catching, cleaning, cooking, and bragging about fish. He has also published widely in magazines such as *Saturday Night*, *Canadian Literature*, *West*, *Journal of Canadian Fiction*, and others. He has been nominated for five Canadian Magazine Awards, and won two for essays included in *Writing Home*. In addition, he won two Western Magazine Awards for pieces collected here. He lives and writes in Saskatoon, where he has also taught English at the University of Saskatchewan.

This book is for Kever

These essays have appeared previously in the following:

"Writing Home" in *Canadian Literature*
"Geopiety" in *Mosaic*
"The Song of Fritz and Belva Twilt" in *Perceptions* and *Vox*
"Sinclair Ross's Horsey Comedy" in *From the Heart of the Heartland: The Fiction of Sinclair Ross*, edited by John Moss
"Shelf Life" in *West*
"Tyee" in *Western Living* and in *Lakes, Lures, and Lodges* by Jake MacDonald
"Patrified Mummies and Mummified Daddies" in *Settlement of the West*, edited by Howard Palmer
"Nomme de Plume" in *Nimrod* (Oklahoma)
"The Prince and the Pelicans" in *Saturday Night*
"The Darker Implications of Comedy" in *Freelance*
"The Morality Tale of Richler's *The Apprenticeship of Duddy Kravitz*," afterword in *The Apprenticeship of Duddy Kravitz*, New Canadian Library Edition (NCL)
"Homage to Henry Kreisel" in *The Bullet*
"The Word According to Carp" in *Event*
"What We Talk about When We Talk about Carver" in *Descant*, *Western Living*, and *Remembering Ray* (Capra Press, Santa Barbara)
"Spring" in *West*

Writing Home

*Selected Essays
by David Carpenter*

Foreword by Alberto Manguel

FIFTH
HOUSE
PUBLISHERS

Cover photograph by Sean Francis Martin
Cover design by NEXT Communications Inc., Saskatoon, SK

The publisher gratefully acknowledges the support received from The Canada Council, Communications Canada, and the Saskatchewan Arts Board. The author wishes to thank The Canada Council and the Saskatchewan Arts Board for grants received during the revision of this book. As well, he wishes to thank the trustees of the Maclean-Hunter fellowship in Literary Journalism for a Banff Centre residency during the writing of "Hoovering to Byzantium."

Printed and bound in Canada by D.W. Friesen and Sons, Altona, MB
94 95 96 97 98 / 5 4 3 2 1

CANADIAN CATALOGUING IN PUBLICATION DATA
Carpenter, David, 1941–

Writing home
ISBN 1-895618-34-7

I. Title.
PS8555.A76158W74 1994   C814'.54   C94-920000-X
PR9199.3.C37W74 1994

Note: Inconsistencies in style and usage in this collection reflect the different treatments originally accorded the individual essays, reviews, scholarly articles, and ruminations contained herein.

FIFTH HOUSE LTD.
620 Duchess Street
Saskatooon, SK S7K 0R1

Contents

Note: The dates in parentheses following chapter titles indicate the date of final composition.

Foreword

In the year 1670, in a book the Catholic Church was later to describe as "forged in hell by a renegade Jew and the devil," the glass-polisher Baruch Spinoza meekly observed that his reactions as a reader varied greatly. "I remember," he confessed,

> having once read in a book that a man called Orlando Furioso used to ride a kind of winged monster through the air, fly over any country he liked, kill unaided vast numbers of men and giants, and other such fancies which from the point of view of reason are obviously absurd. A very similar story I read in Ovid about Perseus, and also in the books of Judges and Kings about Samson, who alone and unarmed killed thousands of men, and about Elijah, who flew through the air and at last went up to heaven in a chariot of fire drawn by fiery horses. All these stories are no doubt alike, but we judge them very differently. The first one seeks to please, the second has a political purpose, the last a religious one.

I can imagine the old man, sitting among his books in the wintery light of his shop in Antwerp, trying to decide which of them fitted each of the three categories, and finding, with a certain secret shame, several for which he couldn't find any other purpose than that of pleasing.

Less categorical than his remote ancestor ("we all descend from Spinoza," Borges once declared), David Carpenter seems quite prepared to acknowledge that pleasure is the driving force in his readings. In this we are alike. I remember the sacrilegious delight with which, at the age of thirteen, I threw out of a third-storey window an ostentatiously bound novel that a well-meaning neighbour had given me as a birthday present, just because it *didn't* please me. Many years later I came across it in a second-hand bookstore and, flicking through its yellow pages, I was glad to see that I fully agreed with my impetuous younger self.

According to Carpenter, our sense of pleasure isn't arbitrary: It is informed, he tells us, by something other than taste, something that has to do with place and time, something Carpenter calls "home." Spinoza—had Carpenter invited him to discuss *Writing Home* over a coffee at the Broadway Café in Saskatoon—would have agreed, since he believed that time and place are simply the stuff we are made of. I can see a friendship flourishing: Carpenter leading the old philosopher on a Saskatchewan fishing expedition, the one explaining the intricacies of fly-casting, the other demonstrating the influence of Descartes on Raymond Carver.

Writing Home is a richly rewarding collection. To see favourite writers such as Alistair MacLeod and Mordecai Richler intelligently annotated, to be (almost) convinced of the merits of others whom I've never much liked, to be offered the discovery of the (to me) puzzling joys of geopiety and patrification, to be introduced to Georges Bugnet and the anglers of Paradise, to be made to wonder about the imaginative links between Robertson Davies and Iris Murdoch and John Irving—and all this in a clear, sparkling style—is pleasure in the deepest sense.

Those who confuse the pleasures of the essay with academic jargon (like those who confuse the pleasures of fiction with the peculiar behaviour of Aunt Edna or the obnoxious manners of Cousin James) have a bewildering but ultimately misguided faith in literature. Literature, at its best, doesn't define anything; it suggests, it hints, it points. An old metaphor compares the book to the world; an older one still compares the world to a book. Both rely on our intuition (and acknowledgement) that everything we touch, everything we see, is mysterious, and can't be explained away by words or by the senses. The best essays acknowledge that mystery's presence—its shadow, its weight—but don't feel obliged to pin it down with formulas or pseudoscientific vocabularies. In that secretive landscape which is literature's realm, the author is always uncertain. Perhaps it was that very uncertainty that secretly pleased Spinoza, in the days when Carpenter was still to come.

ALBERTO MANGUEL
SELESTAT, JANUARY 27, 1994

Acknowledgements

FOR MORE THAN TWENTY YEARS I have piled up debts to people who have taught me things about writing essays. Their lessons and probably their words ring in my ears to this day. Some of these influences are featured in these essays, but others need to be acknowledged.

One of my very first and happiest influences was Mort Ross, who for his sins was my thesis supervisor. Another good influence was Barbara Moon, who acted as my editor seven years ago at *Saturday Night*. She is remarkable for her vigour, good sense, and enthusiasm. A third influence came from a conversation I had with Brian Crick in 1974 about critics who write in their own maverick voices. One of my most recent influences has been Alberto Manguel, as fine a reader as ever graced either end of the Americas. I have benefitted recently from the editorial advice of Jim Sutherland and even more recently from the advice of my editor for this book, Charlene Dobmeier. A number of my associates in the English Department have also exerted a positive influence on me as an essayist by using words in ways I have admired and learned from. Some of these people have also read my manuscripts and made useful suggestions. Colleagues Calder, Clark, Kerr, Gingell, Findlay, Stephanson, and Stoicheff, thank you one and all.

Introduction

*T*HIS BOOK IS A MISCELLANY of eighteen essays, sixteen of them written over the past eight years. I hope many of you have already discovered that a miscellany can be a thing of beauty. For a long time most of my bookaholic friends and I suffered from the fashionable delusion that in unity is strength, which is to say that any collection of writings should be unified around a common theme or motif. What a curious notion. It's time to invite in a little chaos and admit that in diversity is our strength. When we write a poem or a story, surely we don't stop to consider if our piece fits a prearranged scheme. Or when we choose from our poems or short stories to plant them in that sacred little garden called a book, surely we choose our best work and not simply the work that conforms to some grand, all-subsuming marquee called *central concept*.

I write an essay because in a certain month I have stumbled upon something that interests me. My essay will eventually, I hope, arrive at its own particular shape and conclusions because in that month of its conception I allowed it to. So in this collection we have essays of every length and tone and subject matter. All they have in common is that they still please me.

Well, okay. There is something else that binds these eighteen pieces together, a conviction that is too mysterious and vague to be called a thought, much less a central concept: the sense that all reading and writing, all consciousness, is in some way defined by the place we call home. Our original home or an adopted one. I've lived most of my life on the prairies. I've made a lifelong attempt to be in this large place and call it home. I can't read about Iris Murdoch's London except as a man who lives in Saskatoon. I can't write about Georges Bugnet except as a tourist to French culture and language—an informed tourist, I hope, but always an anglophone fellow who grew up on the prairies. Most of my letters are letters home or letters from home. Most of my fiction is about home, a rearrangement of the places I've called home.

The title for this book is taken from a review I did of some stories by Alistair MacLeod. I believe that he is the most natural heir to Ernest Buckler's worthy legacy, and not only because both of them write brilliantly. Like Buckler, MacLeod emphatically *comes from* somewhere, and he has learned how to call that place home. He no longer lives full time in Cape Breton, but when he returns there to write, he returns home.

If, as a nation, we could absorb the wisdom of writers like Alistair MacLeod and find ways of calling our places home, perhaps we wouldn't be so worried about losing so much to free trade, to cross-border shopping, to the forest industry, to foreign fishing boats, nuclear fuel dumps, American imperialism, or global capitalism. People who live in a place and learn to call it home are too vigilant about that place to allow it to pass out of their control.

Most of these essays are given over to book talk. Readers will find reflections on some of our most distinguished writers, such as Margaret Atwood, Robertson Davies, F.P. Grove, Margaret Laurence, Hugh MacLennan, Martha Ostenso, Mordecai Richler, Sinclair Ross, and Guy Vanderhaeghe. Readers will also find essays on people who in my view maintain a strong following in this country and who have had a substantial influence upon Canadian writing (John Irving, for example, Iris Murdoch, Harold Pinter, and Raymond Carver). Some of these essays are nonliterary pieces, familiar essays done for popular magazines. Some of them, like my piece on Fritz Twilt, are heavily fictionalized, but I'm not going to tell you which ones. I like to keep my editors guessing. My personal favourites in this collection are literary (as opposed to scholarly or critical) essays. By *literary* essays I mean those on a literary subject in which the voyage to a discovery is at least as much fun as the discovery itself.

The word "essay" comes from the French *essai* and from the Latin *exagium*, "to weigh" or "drive out, examine." It's well suited to so many causes and modes of expression, to such a wide range of intellect and sensibility, that it seems to have a nebulous meaning these days. It's an undervalued form, a misunderstood genre with a bad rap. Why else would the ungainly term "creative nonfiction" ever have been born? Isn't this a way of saying that most nonfiction is by definition noncreative? Surely the hep wordsmiths who dreamed up this one were never lovers of essays. Surely Samuel Johnson or Annie Dillard or Susan Sontag or Tom Wolfe would have something to say about this limp neologism. As a writer of prose, was George Bernard Shaw ever more alive than as an essayist?

Literary theorists and academics in many disciplines are among the worst offenders against the genre because too often the jargon they choose for their essays is accessible only to a small and privileged group of people who read, more or less, the same books. I have written a great deal about literature in this collection, and I've tried do so in the plain style; but in the earliest of these essays ("Patrified Mummies and Mummified Daddies," written twenty years ago), there should be a red-letter warning for people who are not wildly in love with the professorial voice. I couldn't seem to say my piece without at least a minimum of stiff-rumped academic jargon. This is the only real early piece in this collection. I included it for several reasons. First, it was thought to be such a groundbreaking piece of feminism, that on the basis of this article alone, I was offered a job to teach feminist literature in an eastern university. (I have since been asked not to reveal which university or how many men were on the hiring committee. Ah, those were the days!) The second reason I have included this essay is that it provides an introduction to Georges Bugnet, the scientist/novelist/poet from France who settled in Alberta, and who, alas, still needs an introduction in this country. My last reason for including such an academic piece is that it provides the best evidence I can find of where I came from in my transformation from academic to writer. Since this early piece was published, and many essays like it, I've tried to write about literature less as a critic, theorist, or academic, and more as a reader. But not as a belletrist or a writer of creative nonfiction. You see? We need a better word here.

Essayist? Why not.

I was recently told that hypertext is about to take over from books. Not only are the book and the essay and the story as we know them *dead*, they are about to be replaced by word games on computer in which the reader chooses the sequence of ideas or events in the piece being read. No more linear plot or sequential reading. If you want, you just use your cursor to choose the next thread in a text with many choices. The man who announced this was part of a trio demonstrating the virtues of hypertext to a young, open-mouthed audience of television watchers and a few old farts like myself who admitted to having read books willingly. The three young men who announced this news were conspicuously futuristic. One of them had no last name. (I've never had much luck with people who have no last name. Have you?) One fellow would speak while the other two waited for their moment in the demonstration. The sequence of speakers was orchestrated with corporate exactitude, and I could not escape the impression that I had been beamed into a science fiction movie. As the first speaker was doing his spiel, the other two waited with an expression of mysterious portent, as though awaiting orders from Jean-Luc Picard.

"The book is dead," one of them explained. He was the one who still read things. "It is dead because the computerized texts are more *interactive*."

"What do you mean 'interactive'?" I said. The word felt oddly metallic in my mouth.

"More intellectually involving," said one of the trio. "More nonsequential," said another. "More reader friendly in every way," said the third fellow, the one who read.

I asked him (for he was clearly their leader) if he could name a book he had enjoyed recently. He mentioned several Victorian novels. And did he find these books "interactive," I asked.

"Well," he said, "I suppose so."

I should hope so. For when at last we were treated to a couple of classics of hypertext, I tried very hard to interact. I felt like a retired and overweight bishop trying to learn the twist. The process was about as stimulating as reading the owner's manual to a particularly challenging can opener. It was worse than art gallery prose!

Book talk needs to be liberated from the bastille of experts where too often it languishes in a prison of pseudoscientific jargon. Book talk needs to be restored to the common reader or, if you like, those neighbourhood intellectuals who read omnivorously and who just can't wait to get into a good discussion over the latest book they've read. Their need to discuss books is so great they will form reading circles and book clubs to get the job done. A nation without these zealots is an impoverished place indeed.

Long live the plain style. Long live its flamboyant cousin the baroque flourish. Long live the sentence and all its sparkling possibilities. Long live clarity. Long live the act of weighing, driving out, examining. Long live all the neighbourhood intellectuals who drink coffee at the Broadway Café in Saskatoon and its sister oases throughout the country.

Down with jargon. Down with privileged language spoken to and by specialists who fear clarity. Down with the stifling safety of a specialized vocabulary for those who would speak only to the converted. Down with creative nonfiction. Let us leave hypertext word games to those postliterate futuroids who can afford them. Up with the essay in all its diverse colours.

Confusion to our enemies.

Writing Home *

NOT TO BE CONFUSED WITH MacLeod's first Canadian book, *The Lost Salt Gift of Blood* (1976), this new one contains only four stories from the original, six stories from As *Birds Bring Forth the Sun* (1986), and one haunting new story, "Island." Joyce Carol Oates has edited this volume to launch MacLeod's American debut.

Alistair MacLeod writes about rural life in the Maritimes, and usually about northeastern Nova Scotia. Perhaps I should add, *as he imagines it.* But when he itemizes the agonies of shovelling coal in a bootleg mine, or catalogues the objects that wash up on his particular shore, or describes for us what happens to pack ice on the ocean in late winter, one gets the impression that MacLeod is there, at home, in more than imagination.

In his stories an entire community seems to proclaim itself. In "The Closing Down of Winter," for example, the narrator speaks in the first person plural, almost never referring to himself as "I" or "me." Speaking as "we," MacLeod's narrator is presumably spokesman for a species, the miners on Cape Breton. They may work and die in mines all over the world, but like MacLeod, they most emphatically *come from* somewhere. They belong to the beaches, graveyards, beer parlours, the Gaelic songs, and stories of their own mining community.

MacLeod writes about rural maritimers as only a maritimer can. His years out west and in Windsor have only served to confirm his status as a maritime writer. His characters are

*"Writing Home" is a review of *The Lost Salt Gift of Blood* (New York: Ontario Review Press, 1988) by Alistair MacLeod.

1

farmers, miners, and fishermen and their families. They are largely working class, and when he introduces middle-class characters into his stories (a teacher or TV producer, for example), there is often an uneasy tension between that character and the rural inhabitants. I am not saying, therefore, that the virtues in *The Lost Salt Gift of Blood* are largely sociological or documentary. I am saying that this passionate engagement with place, this evocative rendering of Cape Breton, is vital to the success of these stories *as stories*.

If we look at how he deploys these authentic observations of his region, we see much more than a social historian or a folklorist at work; we see the storyteller firmly in control. In "The Road to Rankin's Point," for example, the narrator, who is terminally ill, returns to the house of his grandmother after a long absence. Both Calum (the narrator) and his grandmother are coming to the end of their lives. Indeed, they will die on the same road Calum's grandfather died on seventy years earlier. Calum states his situation this way: "I have returned now, I think, almost as the diseased and polluted salmon, to swim for a brief time in the clear waters of my earlier stream. The returning salmon knows of no 'cure' for the termination of his life." Calum arrives at the house and describes it. "Entering the porch that leads to my grandmother's house it is necessary to step down. With the passage of the years the house has sunk into the earth. The stone foundation of more than a century has worked itself deep into the soil and now all doors are forced to open inward."

I suppose it is rewarding enough for readers to see through the eyes of a writer who can show them the "diseased and polluted" look of a spawning salmon or what happens to an old frame house by the edge of the sea. But to me the reward comes in the suggestive value of MacLeod's images, the precise way they lie in the weave of his story. Calum's return is indeed almost like that of the diseased and polluted salmon. The waters of his earlier life are comparatively clear, as he rediscovers, but unlike the doomed salmon that might manage to spawn before they die, Calum is the end of his line. He and his grandmother are (to switch images) sinking slowly into the earth. And on this doomed voyage, they are also sinking into themselves, into the past, away from the outside world into a solipsism in which all doors "open inward."

In "As Birds Bring Forth the Sun" and "Vision," written more recently, MacLeod tells his story, then goes on to tell the story about the story, exploring its impact on future generations of maritimers. His narrator of "As Birds Bring Forth the Sun" tells first of the death of his great-great-great-great grandfather, who was attacked and torn apart by a pack of huge wild dogs. People of his own generation are still haunted by the tale and move "like careful hemophiliacs, fearing that they carried unwanted possibilities deep within them."

Perhaps MacLeod's most recent work (stories that investigate and comment upon themselves) aligns him with the metafictionists to some extent. But calling Alistair MacLeod a metafictionist or a regionalist does him little justice. If he is a regionalist, he is not bound by the parochial snares of a limited vision. And if at times he appropriates the structures of post-modernists, he does not succumb to the complacency of the professorial voice that enervates a lot of today's metafiction.

I think the greatest peril he courts in this volume is the one faced by all who write elegiacally about their region; it is the danger that fellow Nova Scotian Ernest Buckler did not always escape. This is the tendency to write with such vigilance about the vanishing rural past that the other world, the urban world most of us inhabit, seems tainted by comparison. And while this may be true in fact or compellingly true in fiction, the elegy tends to lose credibility whenever the tone of moral disapproval invades it.

I must conclude, however, that we could use more writers as probing and compassionate as Alistair MacLeod. His new selection of stories brings to the American audience some very good news indeed. The dozen or so American reviews that I have read are very positive. I am not surprised.

Geopiety

W*ITH SOME EXCEPTIONS, CANADIAN LITERATURE* as a whole reflects a severely qualified, lukewarm affection for the terrestrial home of its authors. As such, Canadian literature could be described as a literature of abandonment, a literature lacking in a sense of geopiety.

According to Yi-Fu Tuan, geopiety is a religious concept. "'Geo' means earth; earth refers to the planet, the globe or its surface vis-à-vis heaven; it is also the soil and, by extension, land, country, and nation. 'Piety' means reverence and attachment to one's family and homeland, and to the gods who protect them. 'Geopiety' covers a broad range of emotional bonds between [people and their] terrestrial home" (11-12). The term geopiety derives from an ancient and sometimes primitive world in which ancestor worship and fertility cults were considered normal, in which a sense of awe was felt for a deity who demanded propitiatory rites. Such rites were reciprocal. While the worshippers *needed* to venerate their gods or their ancestors with sacrifices, the ancestral gods needed this propitiation as a demonstration of loyalty.

In modern times, these gods have receded and nature has lost her (or should one say its) capital N. But something of this filial piety, this reciprocity between god and worshipper, remains. For as Yi-Fu Tuan and many other scientifically grounded scholars remind us, reciprocity lies at the core of intelligent ecology. We can expect to get from the land only what we put into it. To destroy anything in our natural environment is to destroy a part of ourselves.

Geopiety, however, is not simply pagan worship recycled into some modern cult of ecology. It also includes human loyalties. As Tuan explains, "Parents give birth to and succor their offspring, who in turn honor their parents and care for them in old age; nature nurtures men and men owe reverence . . . Piety is the compassionate urge to protect the fragile beauty and goodness of life against its enemies . . . Patriotism is geopiety; remove its exogenous imperial cloak and patriotism is compassion for the vulnerability of one's native soil" (33-34).

An interesting early expression of such geopious sentiments is the speech by John of Gaunt in Shakespeare's *Richard II* (2.1.40-57), for one notes here the way in which Gaunt's love of England involves not merely setting, but embraces the people, their rulers, their ancestors and, by implication, the gods themselves.

> This royal throne of kings, this sceptr'd isle,
> This earth of majesty, this seat of Mars,
> This other Eden, demi-paradise,
> This fortress built by Nature for herself
> Against infection and the hand of war,
> This happy breed of men, this little world,
> This precious stone set in the silver sea,
> Which serves it in the office of a wall
> Or as a moat defensive to a house,
> Against the envy of less happier lands,
> This blessed plot, this earth, this realm, this England,
> This nurse, this teeming womb of royal kings,
> Fear'd by their breed and famous by their birth,
> Renowned for their deeds as far from home,
> For Christian service and true chivalry,
> As is the sepulchre in stubborn Jewry
> Of the world's ransom, blessed Mary's Son,
> This land of such dear souls, this dear dear land . . .

There is in this speech, however, more than just a note of nationalism, that kind which is militaristic and intolerant of people in "less happier lands," presumably part of the "infection" against which England is a "fortress." This vigilant attitude easily becomes distorted from a simple, practical, abiding love of place, to an ambition for a mighty empire. Geopiety has nothing to do with territorial ambitions or pride of empire, where conquest rather than compassion for people and place is the ruling ethos.

In Canada, the most impressive affirmations about place have (understandably) very little to do with imperial conquest or nationalistic utterances. The country is too big and strung-out to be encompassed by an island, a "fortress," or a "blessed plot" metaphor. The sincerest attachments are local, reminiscent of Nathaniel Hawthorne's feeling that "when you try to make it a matter of the heart, everything falls away except one's native state" (456–57). So when Ernest Buckler (*The Mountain and the Valley*), F.P. Grove (*Settlers of the Marsh*), and W.O. Mitchell (*Who Has Seen the Wind*) attempt to make their classic statements celebrating the place of their youth, they all return in memory to a small region within their native province. So does Margaret Atwood in *Surfacing*, an ideal novel for this study because it combines geopiety with a criticism of its absence.

Much of Atwood's childhood was spent in the woods of Northern Québec, and in *Surfacing* her four main characters take a trip there to search for the protagonist's father. The protagonist is nameless, a woman who lost much of her identity during the trauma of an abortion and an ensuing selective amnesia. Midway in the novel she and her three friends encounter a dead heron strung up by its feet on a branch at a portage. The nameless woman asks why they had "strung it up like a lynch victim, why didn't they just throw it away like the trash? To prove they could do it, they had the power to kill. Otherwise it was valueless: beautiful from a distance but it couldn't be tamed or cooked or trained to talk, the only relation they could have to a thing like that was to destroy it. Food, slave or corpse, limited choices; horned and fanged heads sawed off and mounted on the billiard room wall, stuffed fish, trophies" (116–17). She has come to believe, as the ancients did, that each animal corresponds to something inside us. "A part of the body, a dead animal. I wondered what part of them the heron was, that they needed so much to kill it" (119).

The answer to her question comes, I suspect, from Taoist thought, in which the heron bears some iconographic significance. It is a symbol for a particular mode of seeing known as *kuan*. As Allan Watts explains, the heron is remarkable for the way in which it "stands stock-still at the edge of the pool, gazing into the water. It does not seem to be looking *for* fish, and yet the moment a fish moves it dives. *Kuan is*, then, simply to observe silently, openly, and without seeking any particular result. It signifies a mode of observation in which there is no duality of seer and seen: there is simply the seeing. Watching thus, the heron is all pool" (74).

The so-called Americans who kill the heron are incapable of responding to that law of ecology which states that everything in the environment is connected to everything else. Equally reflective of this mentality is the view of people and nature as objects to be consumed. The protagonist's fetus is a thing to be discarded; David's wife, Anna, is a "cunt on four legs"; the many victims in the film David is shooting with his friend Joe are mere images for the camera. The frames on a moving picture film generate the lie that each animal or tree is a thing apart from its setting, an object rather than part of a continuous process.

In her guilt-ridden, hypersensitive state, the protagonist remembers her abortion and temporarily loses possession of her so-called sanity. She has suppressed her feelings for so long that they come back with a vengeance. In an act of atonement she becomes pregnant, or so we are led to suspect. All that is civilized, rational, analytical becomes taboo. She has a vision of the natural world of which she is an organic part.

> The forest leaps upward, enormous, the way it was before they cut it, columns of sunlight frozen; the boulders float, melt, everything is made of water, even the rocks. In one of the languages there are no nouns, only verbs held for a longer moment.
> The animals have no need for speech, why talk when you are a word

> I lean against a tree, I am a tree leaning
>
> I break out again into the bright sun and crumple, head against
> the ground
>   I am not an animal or a tree, I am the thing in which the trees
> and animals move and grow, I am a place (181)

Shortly after this vision, her atonement is complete and her rational faculties restored.

Her problem and its solution are mainstream in Canadian literature. She joins hands with Susanna Moodie, Charles G.D. Roberts's Miranda, Marian Engel's Lou, Martha Ostenso's Judith, and many other women whose isolation in nature evolves into a vigilance over things earthly and a suspicion, as we shall see, of things worldly. In fact this tension between earth and world takes us to the crux of geopiety's central debate, as it manifests itself in Canadian literature. Geopiety is reverence for place and all that that implies. In Canadian literature, however, place has more to do with earth than world, to use Dennis Lee's terms. Earth is often feminine in literature. It is that aspect of the planet which we consign to nature. It is "powered by instinct." World, on the other hand, is usually masculine in literature. It is that aspect of the planet which we associate with civilization. Its language is conscious, often scientific. It acts to control nature.

This cosmology has become a massive metaphor in Canadian literature. If the writer extols the city, s/he is apt to do so at the expense of the town or the farm s/he has fled. More often it is the other way around. The city is villainized. Archibald Lampman's "Freedom" is a good example, as the first three stanzas illustrate.

> Out of the heart of the city begotten
> Of the labour of men and their manifold hands,
> Whose souls, that were sprung from the earth in her morning,
> No longer regard or remember her warning,
> Whose hearts in the furnace of care have forgotten
> For ever the scent and the hue of her lands;

> Out of the heat of the usurer's hold,
> From the horrible crash of the strong man's feet;
> Out of the shadow where pity is dying;
> Out of the clamour where beauty is lying,
> Dead in the depth of the struggle for gold;
> Out of the din and the glare of the street;
>
> Into the arms of our mother we come,
> Our broad strong mother, the innocent earth,
> Mother of all things beautiful, blameless,
> Mother of hopes that her strength makes tameless,
> Where the voices of grief and of battle are dumb,
> And the whole world laughs with the light of her mirth.
>   (63-64)

Here the narrator is fleeing "men" and the world they have created and moving toward the arms of his "mother," the earth. The way world and earth are polarized in this poem into evil, mechanized logos (the archetypal masculine) and good, fertile eros (the archetypal feminine) is extremely black and white. When we leave the city we are also leaving Tartarus, or Lampman's version of it, and falling into an embrace with "all things beautiful." That which is worldly is masculinized and villainized; that which is earthly is feminized and glorified.

In a very important sense, Atwood draws upon this conventional dichotomy to present the dilemma of her surfacer. The young woman's problem seems to have been that she relied too thoroughly on her powers of rationalization (which she associates with her dead father) and too little on inarticulate, intuitive feeling (which she associates with her dead mother). To put it in Jungian terms, the archetypal masculine within her (logos, the horned god) has held sway over the feminine (eros, the woman with the round-moon stomach). In this novel, as in much of Canadian literature, logos is associated with the sun, eros with the moon. When the surfacer conceives her child, eros returns with a vengeance, and with it, the rhetoric of geopiety. The sun sets and the moon rises (161-62). The woman's feelings for other creatures surface.

She feels responsible toward them and therefore toward the place that they come from.

Like almost all of her counterparts in Canadian literature, from Susanna Moodie onward, she returns to so-called reality. She cannot retain her own version of a nature-girl/animal-victim and remain alive, so she puts on her human wrappings and, equipped with a new vision that I would call geopious, she reenters her own time. This new vision has come about through an act of propitiation. In a state of necessary healing insanity, she has reinvoked her parents in order to atone for separation from them and from all the things that mattered to her. Her parents become physical incarnations of the gods. They are, after all, her source of life, her connection to the cosmic sources of life.

Whether one categorizes them as mothers vs. men, eros vs. logos, earth vs. world, or nature vs. civilization, these distinct and separate versions of our place are at war in Canadian literature. Dennis Lee describes it as follows:

> Viewed from the vantage-point of world, there is nothing but world. The bullets, bulldozers, mental structures, rigid moral assumptions and will to power which define the stance of the world . . . are infinitely extensible. Everything on earth is already coloured, charged, configured by the lines of force of world. To be sure, there is still a great deal of raw material strewn about, most of it recalcitrant. But it is all there to be processed into world . . .Yet at the same time, viewed from the vantage-point of earth, there is nothing but earth. A man is himself flesh and blood. Buildings, bodies, brainwaves—everything of world is wholly continuous with the substance of earth. World may be a special case of earth, but it is not in principle different from it. Earth sets about reclaiming its aberrant, hubris-driven civil offspring with an implacable calm, for all the world is earth. The victory is assured . . . Everything that is, is world; everything that is, is earth. Yet at the same time world and earth are trying to destroy each other. (7-8)

In *Surfacing*, the earthly feminine must temporarily assert itself over the worldly masculine before a harmony between the two (the Mother and the Father) can be restored in the surfacer's psyche. Consistent with this assertion of the feminine in the mind of the surfacer is a vigilant, passionate love of nature. Going, then, from *Surfacing* to Hugh MacLennan's *Each Man's Son* is not such a big leap. MacLennan's novel is about Daniel Ainslie, a physician who, in his quest for psychic wholeness, must learn to admire his father less and love his mother more. As in the case of *Surfacing's* protagonist, this psychic readjustment is complicated by the fact that both his parents are dead. And like *Surfacing*, this novel is also about people's attachment to place. The place is Cape Breton Island and men love it as though it were a woman. The novel begins as follows: "Continents are much alike, and a man can no more love a continent than he can love a hundred million people. But all the islands of the world are different. They are small enough to be known, they are vulnerable, and men come to feel about them as they do about women" (193-94). Three women sustain the woman/island metaphor throughout this novel: Daniel's wife Margaret, who by name alone is associated with the Margaree Valley, the idyllic home of Daniel's youth; Daniel's mother, who lived and died on the island; and Mollie MacNeil, who reminds Daniel of his mother.

Daniel Ainslie is the very embodiment of life-denying logos uninformed by and suspicious of the life-affirming wisdom of eros. He must learn some kind of love for his dead mother before he can love either his wife in a meaningful way or the orphan who will become his son. His mentor Dougald MacKenzie tells him, "You would do well to honour your father less and your mother more" (194). As the novel's climax and denouement seem to demonstrate, Daniel succeeds in learning his lesson in love.

Here, in summary, is what happens at the end of the novel. Mollie's boxer husband comes home. By now he is a punch-drunk, ruined man, blind in one eye from too much punishment in the ring. He catches his wife with a lover (Camire, the French revolutionary), and murders them both before falling into a coma himself. This leaves the traumatized little Alan free to be adopted by Margaret and Daniel. The boy cowers from Daniel. Dougald

MacKenzie, mentor to the end, assures Daniel that the boy is merely in a state of shock. " 'But I love the boy,' " Ainslie says, and MacKenzie replies, " 'Yes, Dan. Now I think you do' " (246). As MacLennan's introduction suggests, this novel purports to be about man's love of islands. The island is a woman; the woman is an island. The novel, in the spirit of geopiety, urges upon us a love of the island and its people. But *Each Man's Son* has a serious flaw that goes right to the heart of the book. For lack of a better term I would call this flaw the genteel fallacy; it is most obvious when we look at the book's two Penelope figures, Mollie and Margaret. They both await the return of their Odysseus. Mollie's husband, however, is literally gone; Margaret's is merely preoccupied. Mollie is poor and struggling to raise a child. Margaret is a doctor's wife; her biggest problem is loneliness within marriage. Mollie lives in a slum, the *real* Cape Breton Island; Margaret lives on an estate with a stream flowing through. The Ainslies worry that the mine will pollute their stream. This is a laudable sentiment, perhaps, but a long way from geopiety.

The genteel fallacy puts majestic scenery before people; the most vital works in the geopiety tradition, however, would argue that people and place are inseparable. But in *Each Man's Son* genteel sentiment abounds. MacLennan has made this novel Daniel and Margaret's story even though the suffering of the boxer, Archie MacNeil, and that of Mollie and Alan, is so much more compelling. We see Archie as the old order Odysseus, a warrior of legendary physical strength. We see Daniel as the modern-day Odysseus. He has a genius for healing. His lonely quest for knowledge is truly heroic. Yet the extent of his suffering, when compared to the plight of the people of the island, is dubious; the quality of his love is suspect, even at the end of the novel. Surely the plight of the people served by Dr. Ainslie, whether they live or die, is more momentous than Margaret and Daniel's search for oneness. Surely Mollie's yearning for a husband who is sold to the meat market of prize fighting is more tragic than Margaret's frustrations over her flower arrangements or, indeed, over her loneliness.

There is in fact no viable advocate in this novel for the island and its people. There is, of course, Camire, the French revolutionary. But he is relegated to a minor role and verbally bested by Daniel Ainslie every time they meet. His defence of the plight of the workers is robotlike and doctrinaire. He is at best an ideological voice, and when he is murdered, there is little sense of loss. Ainslie himself is no advocate for the people of this island. He *seems* to care for them, but in the end he decides he must leave them for the betterment of his career. He seems to love little Alan, but his vision of a father-son relationship is disturbingly tied up with his self-important vision of himself. "A man's son is the boy he himself might have been, the future he can no longer attain. For [Daniel], Alan was that boy . . . He saw Alan as a young man crossing the grass of an Oxford quadrangle with young Englishmen as his friends, sitting in the college hall under the portraits of great men who had sat there before him" (187-88).

As for the Cape Bretoners, Mrs. McCuish is an embittered crone. Big Annie McPhee (as a wronged and raped Brunhilde) and Judge McKeegan are figures of pure comic relief (42). Neither is taken seriously. Nor are Red Willie McIsaac and Angus the Barraman. The latter is a charming storyteller when he is not brawling, the big hearted bruiser-raconteur. He is everything a wealthy tourist wishes to see in a Maritime fisherman village. The orderly who rushes the ambulance to the hospital with three dead or dying victims is a mere child (241). So are the fellow hospital workers Ainslie puts down in his temperamental outburst (185, 242). When the wise old Dr. MacKenzie and Ainslie make their pronouncement, "'They're such fools'" (56), we can see what they mean.

Ainslie and MacKenzie address each other, not as man to man, but as seigneur to seigneur. The problem the novel creates for us is that MacLennan has not successfully divorced himself from this same attitude. He addresses us seigneur to seigneur. His elitism has prevented him from discovering the true humanity of his islanders. They are abandoned by their doctor and betrayed by MacLennan.

This, then, is the central problem of his novel. We are led in various ways to value MacLennan's hero for the depth of his human response to Cape Breton's people and to the island. *Each man's son* is Everyman. Daniel Ainslie is Everyman's saviour. He heals physical suffering with remarkable skill. But at the same time we are led to believe that Daniel and Margaret's suffering is more noble than that of the people around them. We are urged to accept the superiority of the Ainslies' quality of *angst* when the impoverished, often jobless, despairing islanders have infinitely more to endure and accept. MacLennan is therefore arguing at cross-purposes with the spirit of his own book. He argues from the perspective of elitism at the expense of each man's son. To this end, Mollie MacNeil's life is sacrificed. *Each Man's Son*, for all its lyrical and loving response to the island, is a failed expression of geopiety. The depth and sincerity of MacLennan's response to the place and its people (especially the women) comes closer to romantic nostalgia than love. His voice is that of the outsider. His arguments for leaving Cape Breton Island are far more compelling than those for staying there.

I should not be too severe with MacLennan on this point, however, for his novel typifies a disconcertingly large number of Canadian novels in which the main characters, just like the novelists who created them, feel compelled to abandon their region for one of greater sophistication. For every Ernest Buckler or Rudy Wiebe there are many more writers of genuine talent who decide that home is a place that finally compels flight. This is particularly obvious in the fiction of the prairies. F.P. Grove's work provides a good example. In the early books, especially *Over Prairie Trails* (1922) and *Settlers of the Marsh* (1925), we have what appears to be a deep, sensuous affection and fascination for the prairie, its seasons, and its people. Love is not too strong a word. But in later books, dating approximately from the death in 1927 of his daughter, this sense of fascination for and loyalty to the prairies gives way to something coldly materialistic and merely intellectual (again, logos uninformed by the wisdom of eros). In *Fruits of the Earth*, for example, we go through the tedium of counting Abe Spalding's fence posts, watching his house crumble, watching his wife grow fatter, reading his school act verbatim, photographing his farm machinery. Grove's prose is tedious; his response to the land is barren. This sense of wonder at the "brief, saturnalian summer of the north" or the "cannonading, sculpting wind of winter" is all but gone. The new settlers are portrayed as coarse and unruly, not genteel enough for the likes of Abe Spalding. (See my essay in this book on F.P. Grove and Martha Ostenso entitled "Patrified Mummies and Mummified Daddies.")

In Martha Ostenso's *Wild Geese,* on the other hand, we have some strong evidence for the geopious in Judith Gare who lies naked on the warm earth and loves it not as her father Caleb does, for what it can earn him, but for its capacity to renew her as it renews itself after the long winter. To Judith the earth is alive. She lies on it, she makes love on it. And it reciprocates. But Ostenso concludes her novel by sending Judith, this magnificent amazon, off to the city to be Sven Sandbo's wife. By domesticating Judith, Ostenso divests her of the energy that made her such an interesting character throughout most of the novel. This ending amounts to an act of aggression against Judith and an abandonment of her terrestrial home.

As For Me and My House by Sinclair Ross is another story of flight from the land, as Philip and Mrs. Bentley flee from one country church to another, from Horizon to Horizon, and finally move to a city. Witnessing their existence as minister and minister's wife in a series of Saskatchewan villages, we get a powerful sense of the numinous, whispering through the land, but its voice is the wind announcing a "blind and uncaring universe" and the "indifference on the part of the deity." Against this force the people appear to be asserting themselves, not worshipping it, not fleeing it either, but intently, toughly enduring it. So when Doc Hunter, in Sinclair Ross's last novel, *Sawbones Memorial,* speculates on God on the night of his retirement, one is not surprised to see Him envisioned as a departed intelligence, a young fellow, still learning, still experimenting, not here but somewhere else, and who has at least momentarily forgotten about us. In His place is "The Great Mother and the Evil Mother, maybe one and the same, creating life only to destroy it" (126). It is little wonder that Mrs. Bentley and Philip leave Horizon and its people, that Doc Hunter leaves Upward to die. These characters seem to be following their Creator's own instincts for flight.

In contrast to Ross's powerful, bleak stories, we find in the best work of W.O. Mitchell a lyrical response to the land; it is evident that the prairie has the power to move him deeply. He even embodies a sort of geopious, ecological morality in the persons of Uncle Sean and his protégé Brian in *Who Has Seen the Wind*. Mitchell's wind in this novel, however, is not the same one that blows through a Ross novel. It is a moral wind, disturbingly moral. When it is roused, it attacks the evil and preserves the good. The Abercrombies' porch is wrecked, Bent Candy's barn is levelled, but St. Sammy's piano box is untouched. One suspects Mitchell's love of his terrestrial home depends upon morally grounded illusions about nature and that the book falls short of a scrupulous engagement with what Mitchell calls "the realities of birth, hunger, satiety, eternity, death." He defends the land eloquently, but to do so, he cheats.

Not so far from Mitchell's Crocus is Wallace Stegner's Whitemud. What Mitchell calls silver willow, Stegner calls wolf willow. These shrubs are Stegner's madeleines soaked in the decoction of limeflowers; they evoke for him and for us his entire boyhood in the Cypress Hills. They bring him home spiritually. Stegner's response to this part of the prairie is no less moving than that of W.O. Mitchell, with whom he shares a strong kinship. But after sharing some rather horrifying scenes of nature's capacity to destroy life in "Genesis" and "Carrion Spring," one is not surprised when this latterday Proust admits, "By most estimates, including the estimates of memory, Saskatchewan can be a pretty depressing country . . . Let it be," he says, " . . . a seedbed, as good a place to be a boy and as unsatisfying a place to be a man as one could well imagine" (306).

Perhaps Margaret Laurence shares some of this ambivalence. Her protagonists certainly do. Though her observations of prairie landscape are authentic, she is less an observer of the natural world than the other writers considered here. She spends much more detail on townscapes, houses, interiors, stores, funeral parlours than on the natural landscape. When she does focus closely on the land, however, there is often a sense of awe and desolation in her response. A good example of this kind of response is in the story "Horses of the Night." When Vanessa looks at the flat, gray, unpeopled shores of her cousin Chris's lake, its reaches passing beyond human sight, "it was like the view of God which [she] had held since [her] father's death. Distant, indestructible, totally indifferent" (148).

An interesting difference between Laurence's characters and those of most of her predecessors is that Laurence's prairie communities, like her characters, are portrayed from the inside rather than from the point of view of the genteel tourist to small town prairie life. Therefore she does not deal in colourful eccentrics, diamonds in the rough, and the many local colour prototypes one associates with Canadian rural fiction. Her characters, especially her women, are memorably, unromantically real. They leave their prairie, but like so many other writers and protagonists, they take it with them, just as their Scottish ancestors did who brought their native Highlands with them to the new world.

The Indian stories of Rudy Wiebe are even better examples of geopiety in action. The old voices speak through his pages. In *The Temptations of Big Bear* these are the voices of the first prairie people and the river people who lived amid the holiness of Sun and Earth and Horse, Coyote, and Bear. Perhaps to his discredit, Wiebe has locked his Indians inside the temporal reservation of pedantic whiteman history, the prison of profane rather than mythic time. They are the inevitable victims of historical determinism, what some people might call progress. But when Big Bear assumes the centre of this novel, dances in the sun, chants the holiness of the immortal Earth, something sane and powerful escapes the prison of history to touch Wiebe's modern, primarily white audience. I was very touched by Big Bear's laments and loyalties in a way that engages my own love and reverence for the earth and its abandoned creatures. In other words, Wiebe responds to the sanctity of earth and sun because he actually believes in it. And Rudy Wiebe, who has never been an exile from the prairie, stands almost alone among prairie writers in his reverence.

The writer's exile from his or her birthplace need not be a rejection of home. In the case of James Joyce, leaving Dublin seems to have been the best way to come to terms with it. This can also be said of Margaret Laurence, Robert Kroetsch, and many other prairie writers. Still, there is a preponderance of stories in Canadian literature in which the main characters discover that the only sensible thing to do in the end is leave home. In Margaret Laurence's *The Diviners*, Morag thinks about leaving home: "You Can't Go Home Again, said Thomas Wolfe. Morag wonders now if it may be the reverse which is true. You have to go home again, in some way or other" (302). Perhaps Morag's return to Canada, but to a place that only reminds her of her prairie home, illustrates something about Canadians' national ambivalence about their native place, their many native places.

The farm or rural community's loss is the city's gain. The Ainslies, Bentleys, Judiths, Rachels, and Hagars leave their terrestrial home (with their creators) for a worldly one. The main characters in *Surfacing* go back to the city. Indeed, much of what I have documented here indicates the movement in Canada from an agrarian to an urban society. So writers like Sinclair Ross, Margaret Laurence, and Hugh MacLennan are, by their characters' movements, in a sense, registering social change.

But what of those Cape Bretoners who remain in the mines, those men and women who remain on the land, those non-tourists to the rural reality? Their story is usually not told, or told as a background to the more genteel and upwardly mobile quests of the adventurous ones who leave.

Sanguine viewers of the Canadian literary scene will no doubt point to the urban writers of the last half-century or so, and demonstrate how the city has become the Promised Land. Montreal is a good example. Some of A.M. Klein's and Leonard

Cohen's best panegyrics (in verse and poetic prose respectively) have been in praise of Montreal. And Mordecai Richler has created a squalid but affectionate monument out of St. Urbain Street. But praising these urban writers (as they deserve to be praised) does nothing to erase the vision we have received from so many writers of our rural past: a series of regions too threatening for proper civilization and culture to survive, wilderness too terrifying to be understood clearly. Atwood's pioneer in "Progressive Insanities of a Pioneer" and Earle Birney's cabin dweller in "Bushed" are not destroyed by the Canadian wilderness; they are destroyed because of the inadequacies of their own vision of it.

I keep returning to the conviction that there is another side to these desolate stories, however skilfully they have been narrated. Reverence for that first place, be it ever so wild; reverence for those first people, be they ever so ungenteel: this takes us close to the heart of geopiety. Wiebe has taken us there in the voice of Big Bear; Buckler, through the eyes of David Canaan; Atwood, with the surfacer's plunge into her own atavistic origins; Lowry, in Dollarton, with his vision of the redeemed world vis-à-vis the inferno; Maria Campbell argues it implicitly in *Halfbreed*; Howard O'Hagan sings and rages geopiety throughout *Tay John*. There are other impressive narratives in Canada's recent past that one could mention, but it would take a very long book indeed to document the number of stories whose response to the terrestrial home is desperately inadequate. What are Canadians to learn about their origins, their place, from a terminally genteel literature that argues for the abandonment of that place? What are they to learn about themselves from books impoverished by their pale affection or downright loathing for their authors' terrestrial home?

Canada derives from the Iroquois *Kanata*, which means village or community. To return to the *Kanata* means to return home. Another rumour persists, however, that Canada comes from the Portuguese *Ca* (here) *nada* (nothing). Nothing here. I believe Canadians still need to learn how to love their place, their many places. Perhaps beneath the looming spectres of acid rain and global warming, this need has acquired an international urgency. I am not talking about flagwaving nationalism or indiscriminate, uncritical self-adoration. And I want to avoid worshipping the rural at the expense of the urban. I am certainly opposed to those attitudes that see Canada as a colony or a place to test foreign weapons or a place where a lot of money can be wrung from the land in a hurry so that one can rush across the American border and spend it all. My plea is for an intelligent, abiding way of calling this place—these places—we inhabit, home.

References

Atwood, Margaret. 1973. *Surfacing*. Don Mills: Paperjacks.

The Complete Works of Nathaniel Hawthorne. 1899. Volume X. Edited by George Parsons Lathrop. Boston: Houghton Mifflin.

Hinz, Evelyn J., and John J. Teunissen. 1979. "*Surfacing*: Margaret Atwood's 'Nymph Complaining.'" *Contemporary Literature* 20 (Spring), 221-36.

Lampman, Archibald. 1960. "Freedom." In *Poets of the Confederation*. Edited by Malcolm Ross. Toronto: McClelland and Stewart (NCL).

Laurence, Margaret. 1974. *A Bird in the House*. Toronto: McClelland and Stewart (NCL).

Laurence, Margaret. 1974. *The Diviners*. Toronto: McClelland and Stewart.

Lee, Dennis. 1977. *Savage Fields*. Toronto: Anansi. (Although I use the terms "earth" and "world" in a slightly broader sense, I am indebted to Lee for several insights into these two contending versions of our planet.)

MacLennan, Hugh. 1971. *Each Man's Son*. Toronto: Macmillan.

Mitchell, W.O. 1947. *Who Has Seen the Wind*. Toronto: Macmillan.

Ross, Sinclair. 1974. *Sawbones Memorial*. Toronto: McClelland and Stewart.

Stegner, Wallace. 1955. *Wolf Willow*. New York: Macmillan.

Tuan, Yi-Fu. 1976. "Geopiety: A Theme in Man's Attachment to Nature and to Place." In *Geographies of the Mind*. Edited by David Lowenthal and Martyn Bowden (New York). Man's attachment to place may be an unfortunate choice of words, because in novels by writers of both sexes, writers as various as Charles G.D. Roberts and Marian Engel, the feminine perspective on geopiety seems more enlightening than the masculine. For a fuller treatment of Yi-Fu Tuan's ideas on geopiety, see *Topophilia: A Study of Environmental Perception, Attitudes, and Values* (Englewood Cliffs, New Jersey: Prentice-Hall,1974), 59-149.

Watts, Alan. 1958. *Nature, Man, and Woman*. New York: Random.

The Song of Fritz
and Belva Twilt

*F*RITZ TWILT DISAPPROVES OF ART, especially the foreign kind with nude bodies and such. Let the Frenchmen have them, is what he says. He disapproves of live theatre, especially if the play deals with tormented folk who talk like the people across the alley from him, swearing and carrying on and all that negative thinking. Mr. Twilt says if people can't be pleasant they should keep their feelings to themselves and that goes double for actors and actresses. There's altogether too much negative thinking and smut in this world. The worst kind is those books that discuss what his wife Belva refers to as "intimacies." They should all be banned and their creators shot. Not that he and Belva disapprove of pleasure. A nice cup of Ovaltine for Belva, a Rambo movie for Fritz, a game show now and then on the television.

Fritz is good at one thing: arousing moral disapproval in the folks around him. In a fifteen-minute coffee break at choir practice he can whip the blandest collection of people into a frenzy of hatred by using phrases like "protecting our children," "family values," and "common decency." And so politicians listen to him.

Fritz likes Bill C-54. Not because it speaks out forcefully against the exploitation of women and children, not because of its obviously laudable intentions. He likes Bill C-54 because, in places, it is so vaguely worded that it leaves a lot of room for people like him to attack. Its definition of what is pornographic is so broad that, for instance, anything written about adolescent sexuality (not just "visual matter") could be prosecuted or restricted. (See Section 138, a-vi and b). This means "any matter or commercial communication" or any "thing," including books displayed (without opaque wrappers) on library shelves. Fritz just has to look at Section 160, items 1-4, and he feels something akin to an . . . well, he gets sort of excited. And the onus of proof is not on those alleging obscenity, but on the accused, who must prove the artistic merit of the work.

Mr. Twilt looks vigilant these days, like a soldier or a hunter. First, he might go for all the glamour and body-building mags in the Shoppers' Drug Mart. Then he'll have a go at the Public Library, then maybe that play at Twenty-Fifth Street Theatre, then maybe that high school production of *Romeo and Juliet*. You know. The one about those teenagers. *Having intimacies.*

Sinclair Ross's Horsey Comedy

I BEGAN READING SINCLAIR ROSS'S WORK around 1970, a bit before the publication of his last story "The Flowers That Killed Him" (1972). At the time there seemed to be a hunt in progress to find our cultural heroes who in turn would articulate for us that elusive thing called The Canadian Identity. The word was out: Return to your roots, scour the countryside, haul those skeletons out of the closet. The grimmer the better. As a graduate student in search of a thesis, I canvassed the bookshelves in search of the most unsparing realism I could find. What I sought would have as many broken teeth as Faulkner's stories, as many corpses as Hemingway's. It would vibrate with existential angst and vomit, just like in Sartre's *La Nausée*. It would seethe with all the trapped futility of Joyce's *Dubliners*. When I found whatever it was I was looking for, I would feel a shudder in my soul and cry, "The horror! The horror!" And it would be politically relevant too.

I became a cardcarrying proselytizer for stark realism, a grim reality snob in the Saskatchewan tradition: grimmer than thou. But was I alone in my glorification of despair, deprivation, and defeat? I think not.

When I came across "The Painted Door" by Sinclair Ross, I knew I had come home. Several other narratives in *The Lamp at Noon and Other Stories* confirmed my discovery: "Not by Rain Alone," "One's a Heifer," and the title story, "The Lamp at Noon." "A Field of Wheat" was powerfully written, but in those days I was like Atwood's surfacer; I was corpse hunting. And as far as I was concerned, "A Field of Wheat" should have ended paragraphs earlier with the dog Nipper lying mutilated on the ground.

I had become a Rosselyte, what critic Mort Ross refers to as the "gladly suffering reader." Looking back at the critics of *As For Me and My House* in this same era, Morton Ross observes, "It is, I suspect, natural for literary critics to recommend books on the same grounds that castor oil is prescribed; the experience is not pleasant, but it may be good for you" (200).

I felt that to be a true Rosselyte, you had to suffer willingly through these stories; that was part of the aesthetic pleasure. And as I intimated earlier, I was not alone. Here is Laurie Ricou, summing up his impressions of *As For Me and My House* and the grimmest stories in *The Lamp at Noon*: "An empty, unproductive, and oppressive existence in an empty, unproductive and oppressive landscape makes an intense fictional impact. The discovery of meaning in this existence . . . makes Sinclair Ross one of Canada's best novelists" (94). And here is Robert Chambers commenting on the same short stories referred to by Ricou: "Many of the finest moments in Ross' stories combine these few elements: menacing nature, lonely humans, a tightening claustrophobia. The dominant mood is one of attrition, with a terrible harmony between the working of wind upon soil and snow and the slow undermining of human stamina and strength" (13).

Rereading all eighteen of Ross's stories has been a disturbing process for me. So has my reading of the dozen or so critics who have done studies of Ross's short fiction. Virtually every major study seems to emphasize what Margaret Laurence refers to as the "lives of unrelieved drabness" (9) chronicled in these stories. Perhaps she speaks for all the Rosselytes in her groundbreaking preface to *The Lamp at Noon and Other Stories* :

> Throughout Ross's stories, the outer situation mirrors the inner. The emptiness of the landscape, the bleakness of the land, reflect the inability of these people to touch another with assurance and gentleness . . . Ross never takes sides, and this is one admirable quality of his writing. Blame is not assigned. Men and women

suffer equally. The tragedy is not that they suffer, but that they suffer alone. (11)

Laurence's remark here seems to speak for all the stories in *A Lamp at Noon*, but she has very little to say about Ross's *other* stories in this volume, the comic pieces: "The Runaway," "Circus in Town," "The Outlaw," and "Cornet at Night." Her sombre essay seems to have set the tone for all subsequent treatments of Ross's eighteen stories, including those published in Ross's later volume, *The Race and Other Stories* (1982). Ross's comic work in the short story is either ignored by subsequent Rosselytes or cast in such a dubious light that the stories seem unduly severe in the critical interpretations. Typical of these readers is Paul Comeau, who claims that Ross's short fiction between 1934 and 1952 is written in "the tragic mode." This position forces Comeau to paint Ross's comic stories with a strangely grey brush. After all, these characters in Ross's lighter work "come from the same pioneer stock and cling to variations of the same dream [as the characters in Ross's grim tragedies]. For example, Martha's ambition to have her children properly educated is realized by Tom's mother in 'Cornet at Night,' mainly because she has sufficient time and funds to maintain an orderly household and supervise his music and Bible studies" (178). Stories like "Cornet," which I now claim to be richly comic, are seen by Comeau as merely less severe reflections of Ross's "hostile environment" (176).

Keath Fraser's essay on Ross's stories is much more perceptive than the studies of Comeau, Djwa, Chambers, Mitchell, Friesen, and McCourt. Like Lorraine McMullen, he devotes some serious consideration to these comic stories—as comedy. And even more than McMullen he demonstrates a rich awareness of Ross's comic talents.

My problem with Fraser's essay is one I've seen practised by most of the Rosselytes: He reads each story within the pervasive context of all the stories in *A Lamp at Noon*. In his treatment of them, the comic stories come across as though they were part of a formally constituted story cycle, such as *Jake and the Kid* or *Go Down, Moses*. According to Forrest Ingram, a short story cycle is "a book of short stories so linked to each other by their author that the reader's successive experience on various levels of the pattern of the whole significantly modifies his experience of each of its component parts" (19). Fraser reads all of Ross's stories in *The Lamp at Noon* "as part of the futility cycle" he claims Ross has established.

> The futile cycle of eking existence from an indifferent world predominates [in] this collection of stories—a kind of rural *Dubliners* in which the same adult impotence replaces a similar childish Araby. Overall, the book spawns variations on the theme of isolation and its haunting melody is unmistakeable . . . These prairie inhabitants . . . can retreat nowhere that is not whirling vainly in an absurd seasonal cycle. (77)

There is nothing wrong with reading these stories as a unified collection as most critics have done. They are unified by their setting and their time. Indeed, two of these stories were altered by Ross to be made into a linked sequence. The two-part story we now know as "Not by Rain Alone" was first published as two stories six years apart: "Not by Rain Alone" and "September Snow." In her pioneering study, *Sinclair Ross* (1979), Lorraine McMullen notes that "For consistency the original names of the man and wife in 'September Snow,' Mark and Ann, were changed to Will and Eleanor (the names of the man and wife in 'Not by Rain Alone')" (53).

Lorraine McMullen's lengthy treatment of Ross's stories has the advantage of allowing some of them their own separate integrity. Reading them as Comeau, or Fraser, or Chambers do, as a unified cycle, occasionally forces these critics into a discussion of the comic stories as though they were written to a theme: the impact of the drought on farm economy, or how farm debt affects interpersonal relationships. These stories deserve to be read as individual works that maintain their own comic integrity without the cloudlike encumbrance of an overall scheme or a theme that prefigures their significance.

One story badly neglected and distorted by the readings of the Rosselytes is "The Runaway." Chambers claims it is one of

Ross's "best stories" (11), but says nothing about it. Paul Comeau seems to think it has something to do with the price of prosperity exacted by the land, and dismisses it. So does McMullen with the passing thought that "Sometimes nature or coincidence works hand in hand with divine retribution . . . In 'The Runaway' Luke Taylor's own meanness and cheating lead indirectly to his own death and that of all his magnificent horses" (49). By grouping "The Runaway" with Ross's truly tragic stories under the theme of "Nature as Impassive Agent," she obscures the story's comic vitality. McMullen and Fraser are better geared to Ross's comic vision than the other Rosselytes, but even Fraser doesn't seem to know what to say about "The Runaway." *

The only critic bold enough to comment on this story is Ken Mitchell. He gives it a page in his book, *Sinclair Ross* (1981). His reflection on the story is only a plot summary, but he does manage to locate it as "a tale of moral justice in the Faulknerian mode" (18). By "Faulknerian mode" I assume Mitchell means the Faulkner of the *Snopes* trilogy. The story's antagonist, Luke Taylor, is a dishonest horse trader who, like Faulkner's Flem Snopes, becomes the richest landowner in the district. And like Flem, he meets his nemesis, dies violently, and not a tear is shed. I like Mitchell's phrase, "a *tale* of moral justice." Perhaps because this story is a tale, it fits less securely into Ross's collection *A Lamp at Noon* than those ones praised by the Rosselytes for their unsparing portrayal of bleak lives. By "tale" I assume Mitchell means a narrative that is not realistic but has its own kind of brilliance and charm. John Gardner is helpful on this distinction between stories like "The Painted Door" and others like "The Runaway."

> The realistic writer's way of making events convincing is verisimilitude. The tale writer, telling stories of ghosts, or shape-shifters . . . uses a different approach: By the quality of his voice, and

* Here are Fraser's only words on "The Runaway": "Sometimes it seems enough that the bad among them are punished (as is Luke Taylor in 'The Runaway' when he dies in his burning barn, and the wife of the man he cheated calls upon her Biblical clichés that justify his death). But when are the good rewarded? Not really ever . . ." (79)

by means of various devices that distract the critical intelligence, he gets what Coleridge called " . . . the willing suspension of disbelief for the moment, which constitutes poetic faith" (22).

Nevertheless the tale writer, like the realist, must document his story from time to time in some way that gives a credibility to his narrative voice. We believe the narrative "not just because the tale voice has charmed us but also, and more basically, because the character's gestures, his precisely described expression, and the reaction of others to his oddity all seem to us exactly what they would be in this strange situation" (25). The reader of "The Runaway," then, is from time to time given proofs (closely observed details of farm life and human intercourse) that generate a compelling sense of reality—however fantastic or illusory.

Ross uses a nameless boy to tell his tale. This boy obviously loves a good yarn. In the heat of the story's climax, thinks the narrator, "I knew that for months to come . . . [this tale] would be listened to" (95). He begins in this fashion:

> You would have thought that old Luke Taylor was a regular and welcome visitor, the friendly, unconcerned way he rode over that afternoon, leading two of his best Black Diamond mares.
> "Four-year-olds," he said with a neighbourly smile. "None better in my stable. But I'm running short of stall room—six more foals last spring—so I thought if you were interested we might work out a trade in steers."
> My father was interested. We were putting a load of early alfalfa in the loft, and he went on pitching a minute, aloof, indifferent, but between forkfuls he glanced down stealthily at the Diamonds, and at each glance I could see his suspicion and resistance ebb. (83)

So far, we have a realistic story grounded in the conventions of verisimilitude. But note how, in the next passage, the narrator's tone and diction modulate when he comes to his description of Luke Taylor's Black Diamonds and their impact on all who behold them:

For more than twenty years old Luke had owned a stableful of

Diamonds. They were his special pride, his passion. He bred them like a man dedicated to an ideal, culling and matching tirelessly. A horse was a credit to the Black Diamond Farm, a justification of the name, or it disappeared. There were broad-rumped, shaggy-footed work horses, slim-legged runners, serviceable in-betweens like the team he had with him now, suitable for saddle or wagon—at a pinch, even for a few days on the plough—but all, whatever their breed, possessed a flawless beauty, a radiance of pride and spirit, that quickened the pulse and brought a spark of wonder to the dullest eye. When they passed, you turned from what you were doing and stood motionless, transfixed. When you met them on the road you instinctively gave them the right of way. And it didn't wear off. The hundredth time was no different from the first. (83)

Note the closely observed detail here, the "broadrumped, shaggy-footed work horses, slim-legged runners," the sort of things one might associate with any group of normal horses. Then note the intangibles, that "flawless beauty, a radiance of pride and spirit, that quickened the pulse," rendering all who saw them "motionless, transfixed." Note, too, the extravagance of the boy's claims, that *all* people were affected by these magic steeds, even those with "the dullest eye."

Luke Taylor's Black Diamonds turn out to be "balky," which means that at unpredictable times, the very worst times even, they will refuse to move. Once again Luke Taylor has triumphed. The boy narrator's mother, who in this story is always right, had predicted Taylor would manage in some way to swindle them. This was her warning to her husband:

"But there are things you can't check. All the years we've known [Luke] has he once done what was right or decent? Do you know a man for twenty miles who'd trust him? Didn't he get your own land away from you for half what it was worth?" And she went on, shrill and exasperated, to pour out instance upon instance of his dishonesty and greed, everything from foreclosures on mortgages and bribes at tax and auction sales to the poker games in which, every fall for years, he had been fleecing his harvest-hands right after paying them. (86)

We have in Luke Taylor, of course, the classic villain of romance. Caleb Gare comes to mind as well as Flem Snopes. And Taylor's victims provide an interesting contrast to him in this intensely moral struggle. Here is the boy narrator's description of his father:

> According to his lights my father was a good man, and his bewilderment [over Luke's successful swindle] was in proportion to his integrity. For years he had been weakened and confused by a conflict, on the one hand resentment at what Luke had done and got away with, on the other sincere convictions imposing patience and restraint; but through it all he had been sustained by the belief that scores were being kept, and that he would live to see a Day of Reckoning. Now, though, he wasn't sure. You could see in his glance and frown that he was beginning to wonder which he really was: the upright, God-fearing man that he had always believed himself to be, or a simple, credulous dupe. (88)

The boy's father is in fact in the throes of a spiritual crisis that has been precipitated by envy. His envy is not simply for Luke's handsome greystone house and hip-roofed barn, the "abode of guile" as the narrator calls it, but for a much deeper, more forbidden envy, focused on Luke Taylor's Black Diamonds but eating away at the soul of the boy's father. So when he trades his four fat steers for the team of Diamonds, he and his wife are suddenly, mysteriously young again. Our narrator explains it this way: "My father had a team of Diamonds, and my mother had something that his envious passion for them had taken from her twenty years ago" (86).

Seen on its own terms, then, "The Runaway" is a tale told by an ideal teller in the (slightly) hyperbolic tradition about an upright man in danger of losing his soul to a comic embodiment of the devil. Had Ross taken his hyperbole much further, he would have had a yarn in the tradition of "The Devil and Daniel Webster" or "The Black Bonspiel of Wullie MacCrimmon." But like William Faulkner's narrator Ratliff of *The Hamlet*, Ross's narrator reins in on his hyperbole so that on the surface, for the most part, this moral conflict remains fairly realistic. I say *fairly* realistic. Note how, even in realistic passages, the innuendos spread like superstition throughout the narrative. Here is an example. The boy's father loses his hat in a gust of wind. Just as Luke Taylor approaches on horseback, the father reins in his new team of Diamonds so that he can retrieve his hat.

> And after weeks without a single lapse, that had to be the moment for [the Diamonds] to balk again. Was it the arrival of Taylor, I have often wondered, something about his smell or voice, that revived colthood memories? Or was it my father's anger that flared at the sight of him, and ran out through his fingers and along the reins like an electric current, communicating to them his own tensions, his conflicting impulses of hatred and forbearance? No matter—they balked, and as if to enjoy my father's mortification, old Luke too reined in and sat watching. "Quite a man with horses," he laughed across at me. "One of the finest teams for miles and just look at the state he's got them in. Better see what you can do, son, before he ruins them completely." And then, squinting over his shoulder as he rode off, he added, "I'll tell you how to get a balky horse going. It's easy—just build a little fire under him."
>
> "I wouldn't put it past him at that," my father muttered, as he climbed down and started to unhitch. "Being what he is, the idea of fire comes natural" (91).

Just as envy of Luke Taylor's Black Diamonds has apparently robbed the narrator's father of his virility, so too have the horses responded, apparently, to his spiritual conflict, "his conflicting impulses of hatred and forbearance," by humiliating him. And we are teased, rather than informed, to wonder at the cause of this humiliation: a man to whom the idea of fire "comes natural."

If we read Sinclair Ross critics and not this story, we might at this point be tempted to predict the ending of "The Runaway." Will Christian forbearance and God-fearing piety win out over evil? Will the devil (or his emissary) and his demonic charges be destroyed on a Day of Judgement? Of course not. Ross's blind and uncaring universe, the indifference of his deity, which critics often associate with all of his early work, all these resolutely bleak emanations from an absentee or uncaring God will determine the fate of Ross's God-fearing family. Sandra Djwa puts it very well when she says the following: "Because this conflict is intimately connected with the struggle for survival, the tragedy of these stories is that there is often no possible reconciliation of any kind. When an author's horizon is composed of 'the bare essentials of a landscape, sky and earth,' there are no compromises open: if land and weather fail man, the struggle for survival can only end tragically, the extent of the tragedy being largely determined by the strength of the person concerned" (51).

But this is not what happens in "The Runaway." It is not even close. What happens is that Luke Taylor is destroyed, along with his demonic horses, in an inferno. No tears are shed, not even for the horses, and there is only a perfunctory sort of mourning after this apocalyptic incident. In fact, Luke Taylor's death is rather funny. His advice to the narrator and his father is Luke Taylor's undoing. The horses balk again on a cold and windy November afternoon with a load of straw. And this time, exasperated, the father says to his son, " . . . I think I'll take old Luke's advice, and see what a fire will do." The narrator tells it this way:

> I closed my eyes a moment. When I opened them he had straightened and stepped back, and there on the ground between the Diamonds' feet, like something living that he had slipped out of his coat, was a small yellow flame, flickering up nervously against the dusk.
>
> For a second or two, feeling its way slowly round the straw, it remained no larger than a man's outspread hand. Then, with a spurt of sparks and smoke, it shot up right to the Diamonds' bellies.
>
> They gave a frightened snort, lunged ahead a few feet, stopped short again. The fire now, burning briskly, was directly beneath the load of straw, and even as I shouted to warn my father a tongue of flame licked up the front of the rack, and the next instant, sudden as a fan being flicked open, burst into a crackling blaze. (93-94)

The Diamonds bolt, the boy jumps on his entirely ordinary

horse Gopher, and the chase is on. "Riding close behind, my head lowered against the smoke and sparks, I didn't realize, till the wagon took the little ditch onto the highway at a sickening lurch, that the Diamonds were going home. Not to their new home, where they belonged now, but to old Luke Taylor's place" (94).

Note how our narrator has personified the fire, with its nervous flickering, "like something living." Note too how the narrator characterizes the Black Diamonds in Luke Taylor's stable. When the flaming wagon is drawn home by the terrified team, it overturns and sets fire to Luke Taylor's barn. His Black Diamonds are inside, and the boy tries to save them from immolation. Instead of fleeing their stalls to safety, they *all* balk. Instead of being portrayed by our narrator as the innocent victims of an uncaring fate, the Black Diamonds are presented to us as monsters. The narrator describes them as follows:

> I ran forward and squeezed in past [the] heels [of the first Diamond I saw], then untied the halter-shank, but when I tried to lead [the horse] out it trembled and crushed its body tight against the side of the stall. I climbed into the manger, struck it hard across the nose; it only stamped and tossed its head. Then I tried the next stall, then the next and the next. Each time I met the same fear-crazed resistance. One of the Diamonds lashed out with its heels. Another caught me such a blow with a swing of its head that I leaned half-stunned for a minute against the manger. Another, its eyes rolling white and glassy, slashed with its teeth as I turned, and ripped my smock from shoulder to shoulder. (96)

This is the point at which Luke Taylor shows up. He heads straight for his huge burning barn, evading those wellmeaning neighbours who try to head him off. He goes through the door. "The same moment that he disappeared, the floor of the loft collapsed. It was as if when running through the door he had sprung a trap, the way the great, billowy masses of burning hay plunged down behind him" (97). It doesn't take long. Luke returns to his element, and the two remaining Diamonds whose fateful trip "home" started the fire, mysteriously return to a prosaically horsey identity. The narrator fears that they will balk again. He "mounted Gopher as usual and rode through the gate ahead of them, but at the first click of the reins they trotted off obediently. Obediently and dully, like a team of reliable old ploughhorses. Riding along beside them, listening to the soft creak and jingle of the harness, I had the feeling that we, too, had lost our Diamonds" (97).

The story closes with the mother (who in this story, as I have said, is always right) and the father (whose judgement is usually questionable where horses are concerned) trying to place their own construction upon the events of the day.

> "It's always as I've said [the mother argues] . . . *Though the mills of God grind slowly, yet they grind exceeding small.* His own balky Diamonds, and look what they carried home to him." She hadn't been there to see it—that was why she could say such things. "You sow the wind and you reap the whirlwind. Better for him today if he had debts and half-a-section like the rest of us."
>
> But my father sat staring before him as though he hadn't heard her. There was a troubled, old look in his eyes, and I knew that for him it was not so simple as that to rule off a man's account and show it balanced. Leave Luke out of it now—say that so far as he was concerned the scores were settled—but what about the Diamonds? *What kind of reckoning was it that exacted life and innocence for an old man's petty greed? Why, if it was retribution, had it struck so clumsily?* (97-98)

These last words, which I have italicized, are the ones Djwa quotes to arrive at her sombre conclusion about this work. "The good man of 'The Runaway' finds himself troubled by God's justice, especially when the scales are eventually weighed in his favour" (53-54). But "The Runaway" does not end with the man's words; it ends with the narrator's response to the impact of his mother's words. Here are the last lines of the story:

> "All of them," he said at last, "all of them but the team he was driving and my two no-good balky ones. Prettiest horses a man ever set eyes on. It wasn't coming to them."
>
> "But you'll raise colts," my mother said quickly, pouring him

a fresh cup of coffee, "and there'll be nothing wrong with them. Five or six years—why, you'll have a stableful."

He sipped his coffee in silence a moment and then repeated softly, "Prettiest horses a man ever set eyes on. No matter what you say, it wasn't coming to them." But my mother's words had caught. Even as he spoke his face was brightening, and it was plain that he too, now, was thinking of colts. (98)

Note how the conversation in this closing scene goes in one way, but how the tone moves like an undertow in the opposite direction away from any possibility of tragedy. And if the father has undergone a spiritual crisis (which might reappear with the birth of Black Diamond colts), so too, perhaps, has Sinclair Ross. To write "The Runaway" he has forfeited that bleak nihilism he has been branded with in all his early work.

In the above reading, I have characterized "The Runaway" as a tale rich in comic detail. It is much less about the fate of a man and his horses that "wasn't coming to them" than about the damnation of a diabolical schemer and his demonic steeds. Luke Taylor's fire unites the settlement in a common cause. His death restores normality and hope to the characters.

A rereading of all of Ross's stories has served to focus my attentions upon his talents as a comic writer. I hesitate to say what kind of a comic writer, because the very moment I make a formulation of his comedy, I will begin to recall stories in his canon that refuse, like Luke's horses, to conform to a theoretically "normal" category. "Spike" has the structure but not the texture of romantic comedy. "The Race" (an excerpt from Ross's novella *A Whir of Gold*) reads like a long joke or a boy's adventure, full of good spirits and friendly contempt for the strictures of the adult world. "A Day with Pegasus," written in what critics would like us to think of as Ross's early black period, is a realistic story about a boy's fantasy life, and it reads a bit like a Miracle Play. "Barrack Room Fiddle Tune" is Ross's only story written in the first person plural, an anecdote about the impact of a farm boy's terrible fiddle playing on a group of army recruits. There is really only one character in this story, so again, it defies easy classification.

"The Outlaw," "Cornet at Night," and "Circus in Town" have all received fair attention from critics. The only thing I would add to the comments I have read is that these three stories work by means of subversion. The subversive victory in each has something to do with a child's attainment of a vision which is antithetical to that of his or her parents. In each case the child manages to invert the value system that oppresses her or him.

It is interesting to note that the comedy in almost every one of these eight stories is inextricably bound up with horses. For example, in "Cornet at Night" the story proceeds with quiet, almost detached irony. Our narrator, Tommy Dickson, has tried to remain obedient to the strictures of his parents' parsimony. His orders for his first ever trip to town alone are to hitch Rock (an old, utterly reliable horse) to the wagon, do the shopping, and bring back a hired man to help his father with the stooking.

> "Mind you pick somebody big and husky," said my father as he started for the field. "Go to Jenkins' store, and he'll tell you who's in town. Whoever it is, make sure he's stooked before."
>
> "And mind it's somebody who looks like he washes himself," my mother warned, "I'm going to put fresh sheets and pillowcases on the bunkhouse bed, but not for any dirty tramp or hobo."
>
> By the time they had both finished with me there was a great many things to mind. Besides repairs for my father's binder, I was to take two crates of eggs each containing twelve dozen eggs to Mr. Jenkins' store and in exchange have a list of groceries filled. And to make it complicated, both quantity and quality of some of the groceries were to be determined by the price of eggs. Thirty cents a dozen, for instance, and I was to ask for coffee at sixty-five cents a pound. Twenty-nine cents a dozen and coffee at fifty cents a pound. Twenty-eight and no oranges. Thirty-one and bigger oranges. It was like decimals with Miss Wiggins, or two notes in the treble against three in the bass. For my father a tin of special blend tobacco, and my mother not to know. For my mother a box of face powder at the drugstore, and my father not to know. Twenty-five cents from my father on the side for ice-cream and licorice. Thirty-five from my mother for my dinner at the Chinese restaurant. And warnings, of course, to take good

care of Rock, speak politely to Mr. Jenkins, and see that I didn't
get machine oil on my corduroys. (39)

All things considered, Tommy didn't do too badly. His only
major deviation from the rule of the adults is to bring home a
trumpet player with slender and smooth white hands to do the
stooking. The young musician's name is Philip Coleman.
Philip, lover of horses, Paul Kirby might remind us. Tommy
cannot keep his eyes off Philip's cornet case, but other than this,
he keeps his enthusiasms and old Rock dutifully reined in—until
Philip takes his cornet out of the case.

> It was a very lovely cornet, shapely and eloquent, gleaming in the
> August sun like pure and mellow gold. I couldn't restrain myself.
> I said, "Play it—play it now—just a little bit to let me hear." And
> in response, smiling at my earnestness, he raised it to his lips.
>   But there was only one note—only a fragment of a note—and
> then away went Rock. I'd never have believed he had it in him.
> With a snort and a plunge he was off the road and into the
> ditch—then out of the ditch again and off at a breakneck gallop
> across the prairie. There were stones and badger holes, and he
> spared us none of them. (46)

Note how, when Philip puts the cornet to his lips and Rock
explodes, the comedy takes off as well, from a nicely modulated
irony in the first eleven pages to a wonderful moment of farce
that effectively destroys the parental hold over Tommy's mis-
sion. The carefully garnered supplies fly out of the wagon, an egg
crate is smashed, items are lost or ruined, and best of all (or worst
of all, depending on your politics), Tommy has been seduced
into a new vision of soaring possibilities by Philip's cornet.

Ross returns again and again in his comic works to these
moments of subversive joy brought about by a young person
whose feelings are catalyzed and released by a horse. Even the
relatively horseless "Barrack Room Fiddle Tune" does this when
the farm boy protagonist jumps a fence to have a conversation
with a horse.

Horses in Ross's work are usually associated with freedom,

self-sufficiency, release, and sometimes male pride. They are the Pegasus vehicles for a child's dream of freedom and adventure. And in a society in which sexual desire is suppressed so relentlessly, the horse is often the adolescent's substitute for a true object of desire. Isabel, the horse in "The Outlaw" and "The Ride," for example, is a temptress. The horse is the trigger for the body's ecstatic release, so a horse out of control (as in Ovid's story about Phaethon or Pindar's version of Bellerophon and Pegasus) is a moment of high celebration in the life of a prairie youth. When I reread my own summary of "Cornet at Night," I can't help but notice how the images I have cast this story in are charged with erotic innuendoes. The story seems to carry this subcurrent.

It is not my purpose here to offer firm value judgements about Ross's comic work. But I have reached the point where I can urge all the Rosselytes to read his eight short comic pieces *as comedy*. Reading these works will remind us most obviously that Ross has unsung talents as a writer of comedy. It does not, as some critics imply, show up only in Ross's later works; it is there right from the beginning.

Also, if we read Ross's short stories without the constrictions imposed by a prearranged scheme, some form of thematic criticism, for example, we can begin to appreciate Ross's subversive sense of the ridiculous, his buoyant affirmations. And best of all, we can rid ourselves of the excesses of the Rosselytes: their insistence upon suffering as a salutary element of aesthetic pleasure.

I have reread these stories after the rise and fall of postmodernism in North American fiction, after the theatre of the absurd, after Beckett and Pinter, after the quest for the Canadian identity when stark realism was an unchallenged orthodoxy, and I am returning to something Shakespeare must have known a long time ago: that a balanced diet of comic and tragic renderings is healthier than a strict regime of one without the other. When I think of modern Canadian works that might fit some acceptable definition of tragedy, I can think of very few: *The Stone Angel*, perhaps, or *Under the Volcano*. Both are written by people who had, by my reckoning, a pretty good sense of humour. So did Sinclair Ross.

References

Note: Journal articles without page references are cited directly in the text.

Chambers, Robert D. 1975. *Sinclair Ross and Ernest Buckler.* Montreal: Copp Clark Publishing and McGill-Queen's University Press.

Chapman, Marilyn. 1984. "Another Case of Ross's Mysterious Barn." *Canadian Literature* 103 (Winter): 184-86.

Comeau, Paul. 1984. "Sinclair Ross's Pioneer Fiction." *Canadian Literature* 103 (Winter).

Djwa, Sandra. 1971. "No Other Way: Sinclair Ross's Stories and Novels." *Canadian Literature* 47 (Winter).

Fraser, Keath. 1970. "Futility at the Pump." *Queen's Quarterly* 77 (Spring).

Friesen, Victor. 1976. "The Short Stories of Sinclair Ross." *Canadian Short Story Magazine* II, 2 (Fall): 71-73.

Gardner, John. 1985. *The Art of Fiction.* New York: Random House (Vintage Books).

Hamilton, Edith. 1969. *Mythology: Timeless Tales of Gods and Heroes.* New York: Mentor.

Ingram, Forrest L. 1971. *Representative Short Story Cycles of the Twentieth Century: Studies in a Literary Genre.* Paris: Mouton.

Laurence, Margaret. 1968. "Introduction." In Sinclair Ross, *The Lamp at Noon and Other Stories.* Toronto: McClelland and Stewart (NCL).

McCourt, Edward A. 1970. *The Canadian West in Fiction* (Revised). Toronto: Ryerson.

McMullen Lorraine. 1979. *Sinclair Ross.* Boston: G.K. Hall.

Mitchell, Ken. 1981. *Sinclair Ross: A Reader's Guide.* Moose Jaw: Coteau Books.

Moss, John. 1974. *Patterns of Isolation.* Toronto: McClelland and Stewart.

Ricou, Laurence. 1973. *Vertical Man/Horizontal World: Man and Landscape in Canadian Prairie Fiction.* Vancouver: University of British Columbia Press.

Ross, Morton L. 1978. "The Canonization of *As For Me and My House*: A Case Study." In *Figures in a Ground.* Edited by Dianne Bessai and David Jackel. Saskatoon: Western Producer Prairie Books.

Ross, Sinclair. 1957. *As For Me and My House.* Toronto: McClelland and Stewart.

———. *The Lamp at Noon and Other Stories.* 1968. Toronto: McClelland and Stewart (NCL).

———. *The Race and Other Stories.* 1982. Ottawa: University of Ottawa Press.

Whitman, F.H. 1982. "The Case of Ross's Mysterious Barn." *Canadian Literature* 94 (Autumn): 168-69.

Shelf Life

W<small>OULDN'T IT BE NICE</small> if there were a keeper of lost memories? Well, never fear. I have just found him. His name is Stan Foster, son of the late Edward Foster. Stan runs the general store in Borden, Saskatchewan (population two hundred), fifty kilometres northwest of Saskatoon.

It's a hot day, and I walk sweating into a cool fragrance of long ago. The first thing I smell is oiled hardwood floors. The first thing I hear is the clink and hum of coolers. One for Dixie Cups and Revellos, one for pop. Remember those pop coolers, the bottles of Coke and 7-Up kept clinking in cold water, day after sweltering day? And what's for sale in the gloom of the store is far more than I can describe or photograph. Dry goods in one corner—that's clothing, if you're not in the trade. Hardware in another, everything for the lover of gadgets. Food near the entrance and, a little farther down, just this side of dry goods and hardware, several shelves of drugstore items, including some tubes of Brylcreem. Remember?

> *Brylcreem, a liddle dab'll do ya.*
> *Brylcreem, y'look so debonair.*
> *Brylcreem, the gals will pursue ya.*
> *Simply rub a little in your hair.*

The sign reads EDWARD FOSTER. Built in 1909, this emporium is almost as old as the province. On the outside it looks like every general store I've ever seen in the rural west: a simple two-storey frame building painted white, with a tall broad façade that makes the store seem larger. But on the inside, something funny happens to the merchandise. *It never entirely disappears.* Like the souls of the righteous, unsold goods simply rise to the higher shelves where, as if by mercantile magic, they are transformed from commodity to antique.

You notice this as soon as you look up from the shelves to the boarded ceiling. In dry goods, you get farm wear: work shirts, wool socks, and boots. But in dry goods heaven, only a metre higher up, you get whalebone corsets and high-button shoes, straw boater hats and skates that screw into the boot—and I mean pre-Gordie Howe skates.

Try the same exercise in the food section. The bottom shelves contain basic staples: canned goods, pasta, candy, and huge bags of pet food. But up top, it's large tins of Blue Ribbon coffee and Paulin's biscuits, Pictou Twist Chewing Tobacco, and dusty Coca-Cola bottles selling long ago for twenty-five cents a six-pack, a large tin of corned beef for thirty-seven cents, a tin of sardines for five cents. Sardines from 1937. I wasn't able to check if the tins contained the food they were supposed to, because they were too high up. In fact, I didn't *want* to check them out. I was too far into the illusion of recaptured memories to want to disturb them. You get the same variety at Safeway or Supervalu in Saskatoon, sometimes even the same brand names. But there the hardware and children's toys are displayed in cardboard and plastic packages in a disturbingly insular way. Come-hither packaging but hands off the merchandise, like sex in the fifties. The sound of Muzak and the smell of planned obsolescence insinuate themselves like propaganda into the air.

Call me hopelessly old-fashioned, terminally elegiac, but I'd rather have Mr. Foster's clinky water coolers full of Coca-Cola and Orange Crush and hear the radio voices in his old wooden cabinet blare out country and western music as I did yesterday in Borden, Saskatchewan. As I did every summer in Kapasiwin, Alberta, and Fairmont Hot Springs, British Columbia, three to four decades ago.

There is no air conditioning. The prairie wind blows poplar fluff and the smell of clover and hay through the open back door, down the cool dark aisles, and out the front door. You call for assistance beneath a shelf of Union Jacks and other royalist flags, and you get Stan Foster right away. He not only finds the tube of Brylcreem you just have to buy, but in the process gives a brief history of the district. All around you are the items that delineate the needs of the community. All above you are the objects that delineate the community's past. The past has not escaped; it participates in the present. Cans of Off! on a shelf just beneath a big tin of Tanglefoot Fly Spray. Mr. Foster has almost everything I ever bought in a country store when I was old enough to have an allowance. He presides quietly over my memories—indeed, he takes much better care of them than I have been able to.

I leave the store clutching my tube of Brylcreem like an elixir of youth, humming that song all about adolescent potency. *Brylcreem, a liddle dab'll do ya.*

Was it just a faded ad for Tanglefoot Fly Spray or a tin of the real thing? I don't want to know. I feel too good today. I have never looked so debonair.

Tyee

You MAY NOT BE AWARE OF THIS, but all across North America there is a club for sexually disabled fishermen (Sexually Disabled Anglers International). When you join up, the High Archon introduces you and you offer testimony to the fellows in the clubhouse. I haven't been a member for very long, but already I can see that *we all tell just about the same story*. It usually starts something like this:

"Speak, Brother," the Arcon says.

"My name is Bob Loblaw and I have a problem. It all started when I took the wife out for a quick troll before dark. I hadn't caught a fish in three days an' she ties into this big pike, hauls 'er in . . . "

And here's the moment we all start to nod in recognition.

" . . . and this lunker she brought in, it weighed twenty-nine pounds. Bigger'n any pike I ever seen let alone hauled in myself."

There will be murmurs of sadness from the anglers in the room. Moans of consolation. And then the sad confession:

"Ever since that night, well . . . me an the wife . . . "

"Say it, Brother," cries the Archon.

"Well, let's put it this way," the poor man might conclude. "You can't shoot pool with a rope."

My name is David Carpenter and I have a problem. After my testimony at the SDAI an old fellow came up to me and asked me to elaborate.

"It was a rainbow trout," I told him. "Seven pounds twelve ounces. Huge. She took it on a fly. I offered to bring it in for her, and she gave me this . . . "

The old fellow shot me a look of recognition. "Withering look?"

"That's it! A withering look!"

"Why not go out an' catch one bigger? Up north the lake trout go fifteen-twenty pounds regular."

I shook my head. "My wife, she's a purist. I brainwashed her. It's got to be something real jumpy, sporty. And it's gotta be light tackle."

"Then why don't you go for a tyee? That'd do the trick."

"A tyee?"

I've never believed in guardian angels; I don't even believe in good luck. I'm from Saskatchewan. So imagine my surprise when, shortly after the above conversation at the SDAI clubhouse, the phone rang. Jim Sutherland of *Western Living*. "How would you like to catch the biggest salmon you have ever seen? I need a writer/angler."

"You mean . . . catch a . . . "

"That's right," he said. "A tyee."

Tyee is the Salish word for "chief." When a spring salmon (sometimes called chinook) gets to be thirty pounds or better, it becomes a tyee. In British Columbia an entire corporation has been built on this big fish, and its most illustrious fishing camp is Painter's Lodge in Campbell River. This lodge is a mile or so from the Tyee Club, the spiritual home of the most venerable salmon derby in Canada. For almost a century, VIP anglers from all over the world have been coming to Painter's Lodge, a sort of Taj Mahal of fishing camps. Their desire is to catch a tyee and then join the club. The King of Siam, Glen Ford, Zane Grey, Bob Hope. All have come here around the end of August to distinguish themselves in that utterly primitive fashion: killing a mighty salmon.

One of the keenest anglers is the manager of fishing operations at Painter's Lodge, Wayne Dreger. He speaks with the nervous energy of a dynamite blaster, and when he describes the technique of striking a tyee, his entire body seems to tense up like Boris Becker before a serve.

"You watch that rod tip," he says. "You don't take your eyes off it. You may want to talk to your buddy, but that doesn't mean you can take your eyes off your tip. Remember, this is not fun. It is utter concentration. The very second your tip flutters, you strike as though your life depended on it."

My buddy for this trip is an old friend and photographer from Vancouver, Pete Nash. Already he has located our guide and rower, a young man named Randy. He tells us to be ready the next morning by 5:15. Nash doesn't know that I am here for another more urgent reason.

A wakeup call at 4 A.M. Nash and I drift outside in a west coast wooze of fetal memories. Randy is out on the wharf. We are going fishing. As they say out here, we are going to row a tyee.

The Tyee Club rules state that fishermen must not use a motor while fishing. Our rowboat has a motor, but we can only use it to get out to the Tyee Pool. Nash mans the motor while our guide Randy gets the tackle ready. We are using seven-foot rods with single action reels, twenty-pound test line, and large Gibbs-Stewart spoons. Randy is forever shining these spoons as though they were pieces from the royal family's tea service. Randy is obviously the right man for this job. In many ways an ordinary guy, in matters of angling, he is a perfectionist.

We skim over the chuck and the night begins to lift out of the estuary. Shapes loom out of the dark: islands, rocks, hills. We have entered an outdoor gallery of Toni Onley sketches that drift out of the twilight in a dream of yammering gulls. Randy waves a hand at Nash to cut the engine.

My rod tip bobs up and down with the dodging rhythm of the spoon. I hold my thumb on the spool of my single-action reel. When the rod tip flutters, I will not feel the strike. But I will strike back nonetheless. I will yank that thing back so hard I will almost break the rod or my back. Nash is thinking the same thoughts, I am sure. Grim. We are a disciplined duo and we are not—no absolutely not—having fun. Neither the gentle weather nor Randy's unfailing good humour will alter our Prussian demeanour.

"Nash, having fun?"

"Nope."

"Good."

"How about you, Carp? Having fun?"

"Nope."

"Good."

Our first shift ends around 8:30. Just as we are turning to go for breakfast, Randy looks up from his polishing of my spoon. "Dave," he says, "did you feel anything out there this morning? Even a nudge?"

"Not a thing. Why?"

"There's a tooth mark on your spoon."

In five days, about five hundred keeners rowed the Tyee Pool. Not one tyee was killed. We saw them though, rolling out of the ocean like economy-sized orcas or slapping the surface with their tales. They were there, huge and beautiful, too huge to imagine lying comfortably in our small boat. Too beautiful to imagine dead, a mere trophy emblematic of some guy's manhood. Even *my* manhood, which I had almost forgotten about. Seeing the big salmon roll made me wonder. Like the keenest anglers in the Tyee Club, I am trying to kill this creature I admire so much—not by purchasing a tin of salmon in the K-Mart or any other act of consumer boredom—but by fooling it with my patience and my art. Killing a mighty fish is not a moral act; it is a primitive act. Don't be fooled by the cane rods and the tweed coats worn by the old anglers of the Tyee Club. Yes, they are gentlemen, but when they take or harvest or beard or finesse a salmon, the verb they use is "kill." Killing a mighty salmon takes us back, however briefly, to our most primitive origins when fishing well meant eating well. The man or woman beholds the creature helpless and flopping in the boat, beholds how fat and deep the body, how silver the sides, how perfectly streamlined the salmon for long runs and mighty leaps. It may be the first angler at the dawn of time who looks at the fish and says, "Tyee."

Well, Nash and I were skunked. Randy offered us a frozen salmon but (having, I suppose, our pride) we turned him down.

My adventure has a postscript. Alone in my car on the last leg of my journey back to Saskatoon, I had a strong urge to throw out the old fly line. I did a little detour to a lake known for its bruiser rainbows. I had no boat but I knew of a spot where you can flycast from shore without your backcast getting fouled. It was a beautiful day, but this time there wasn't a person in sight. Why is it that these moments come invariably when your photographer buddy and all witnesses are miles away?

Well, I guess you know what happened. On the first cast from shore my fly landed about thirty-five feet in front of me. I waited while it bobbed on the surface, then pulled it under and began to jerk the big fly toward shore. There was a monumental surge where my fly had been and I saw a dark back and the flash of a big dorsal. My reel was buzzing and my fly was being carried at violent speed toward the centre of the lake. When I checked the first long run, the rainbow swam right for me and I had to strip in line as fast as I could. Then the fish wheeled and did a slow leap out into the blue terrific sky. It seemed to hang there in defiance of gravity and reenter as softly as an otter sliding into a pool. I think it fair to say that this too was "Tyee" in another one of his magnificent guises. The Chief had come to call.

It took about fifteen minutes to tire the fish and about five more to head it into a shallow channel where the canoes are launched. Two feet long, as deepbodied as its Pacific cousins, and built for power rushes and acrobatics. A ten-pound rainbow trout. These are about as common as large emeralds in your back garden. It might come as no surprise to my readers that I released this fish without hesitation. Who was I, after all, to presume to spill the blood of the Chief? Unhooked, the fish lay stunned and exhausted in the channel, righted itself, and with a shudder from its powerful tail, ploughed away from the shallow water leaving an impressive wake behind.

I had a very pleasant drive across the prairie all the way to Saskatoon. I had only one lingering doubt in my mind. When I walk into the kitchen with an empty cooler and tell my wife, Honor, that I just released the biggest rainbow either one of us has ever seen, will she believe me?

I love those forlorn fishermen at the old SDAI clubhouse. How I shall miss them.

Patrified Mummies
and Mummified Daddies
Matriarchs and Patriarchs in Prairie Fiction

ONE OF THE MOST DISTRESSING FAILURES in prairie settlement fiction during the first third of this century was the shallow treatment of man and woman living together. It is a subject we expect to find at the heart of a novel. In the *romans du terroir* of western Canada, we find evidence that men and women did actually *live* together. But if the fiction of Nellie McClung, Ralph Connor, R.J.C. Stead, Arthur Stringer, and their more distinguished successors such as Grove and Ostenso, are true reflections of what really happened between man and woman, one wonders why the whole institution of marriage on the prairies was not given up as a grotesque mistake.

It has been fashionable for some time to accuse prairie writers of prudery. This charge is most often levelled at the earliest generation, the one beginning with Ralph Connor and ending with Nellie McClung and R.J.C. Stead. Examples abound. In Connor's *The Sky Pilot* (1899) the hero is a minister who wishes to gain the trust and save the vagrant soul of an unruly girl named Gwen who was thrown from a horse and paralysed from the waist down. Her favourite spot is a canyon. Time after time, in his astounding innocence, Connor describes his heroic crusader lancing boldly through the lips of Gwen's canyon, a canyon lined with wild maidenhair.

Throughout the course of Connor's story one becomes aware

of his reticence to discuss women in anything but stiff or saintly terms. He mentions that Gwen is "not beautiful" so many times it sounds like a nervous tic. It is not a huge leap from that realm of frozen chastity to the premise that Connor is displacing certain creative energies. What he has not acknowledged to his readers (and likely to himself) about the nature of normal male-female attraction, he displaces into other areas of his characters' experiences. And the minister's love for the girl finds expression in the erotic imagery of the girl's canyon. Thus a fearful reticence to explore experience through normal channels results in Connor's perverse displacement of human love and passion.

A more germane example of the perverse displacement of male passion comes in R.J.C. Stead's finest novel, *Grain* (1926). Gander Stake, the main character in the novel, undergoes one of his significant rites of passage into manhood. Unable to win completely the favour of his girlfriend, Jo Burge, unable to prove his manhood by choosing to go to war, he is nevertheless allowed to graduate from driving a binder on his father's farm to driving a straw-burner for a large threshing crew. Gander "loved his engine and delighted in its company . . . The throbbing of the steam exhaust for a time beat down that inner throbbing which could be quietened but could not quite be killed" (98). Disenchantment over his love for Jo Burge can be partially overcome through his attachment to this new mechanical bride. The machine is like an insatiable concubine who comes to life

> at the end of the stroke; the steam entered the forward end of the cylinder; the wrist-pin bearings clicked almost imperceptibly with the reversal of the pressure, and the driving-arm lunged backward with a sharper and accelerating hiss. She was away! Gander let her ramble gently for a few revolutions while the exhaust beat its pleasant tattoo inside the stack, then slowly gave her more steam while he watched the quickening flywheel and knew the thrill that comes only to those who hold great power in the hollow of their hands. Jo Burge? This—this power—this mighty thing that sprang at his touch—this was life! (101)

A moment later Gander's boss yells, "Give 'er juice!" And the chapter concludes with Gander riding his straw-burner to glory: "This was Gander's day of romance. Not that he knew it for that—but who knows Romance when he meets her in the daily round?"

This passage is the closest Stead ever came to an erotic *tour de force*. While it is difficult to ascertain how conscious Stead was of the sexual connotations of the above passage (my guess is he was not remotely aware of them), it is obvious that he was very much at home in the description of machinery and of the masculine enthusiasm over such machinery. But we're left with a novel in which the only explicit scenes of passion are between a boy and his straw-burner. There is a brief, three-sentence splurge of terrified, abbreviated passion on page 165 for anyone unfortunate enough to be keeping track, but that is the only exception.

I stated earlier that it has become fashionable to accuse the first generation of prairie writers of prudery. But such a line of criticism is only a beginning. It would be fairer to approach this malady in our fiction as an imbalance between two allegiances, Eros and Logos, two very old symbols for the archetypal feminine and the archetypal masculine.

First, my terminology must be clarified. Logos refers to that psychic disposition which primitives, poets, and psychoanalysts alike have often associated with the sun, the sun god, and by extension with war deities—that impulse which succeeds by conquering. Logos and nature are always contending for mastery. Whether through social conditioning or not, the power of Logos is usually considered a masculine trait and Eros a feminine trait. Eros is not only a goddess of love and fertility; it is often associated with wisdom, but a much higher, deeper wisdom than Logos. This is an instinctual or intuitive wisdom that, though it lies often beyond the reach of words, seeks oneness and harmony with nature. Neither of these traits is the exclusive domain of one sex. We are, after all, the children of mothers and fathers. But in patriarchal societies, men are encouraged to reflect Logos, women Eros, whether or not this is a natural thing to do.

When Gander Stake, in Stead's *Grain*, diverts his amorous frustrations into his mastery of the straw-burner, we see a good example of Logos without the informing wisdom of Eros. This episode points to an emotional impoverishment that weakens the artistic fabric of some of our most distinguished fiction on the prairies between 1900 and 1935. Even in the best of this fiction one sees an overwhelming number of cases in which the novels' rhetorical allegiance rests too exclusively with masculine forces (Stead, Connor, Grove) or feminine forces (McClung, Stringer, Ostenso) to give a balanced picture of man and woman. Before the publication of our finest *romans du terroir* by such later writers as Christine van der Mark *(In Due Season)*, Gabrielle Roy *(Where Nests the Water Hen)* and Sinclair Ross *(As For Me and My House)*, the subject of man and woman was a sort of dark mystery to be avoided if at all possible. If not, it was usually sentimentalized in the extreme.

Stead's character portrayals of women are typically lifeless and unconvincing. One of his heroes, the writer Calvin Beach, who dominates both *Grain* and *The Smoking Flax* (1924), could be stating Stead's own credo when, in the latter book, he says, "Every human soul . . . is an engine which *will* go; the thing is to put it at useful work and save it from blowing itself, and others, to pieces" (27).

This mechanistic attitude to human life is another good example of Logos uninformed by the wisdom of Eros. And since there is no evidence to suggest Stead does not support this attitude to human character (this credo is championed by the protagonists of both novels), it helps to explain the lifelessness of most of his character creations, especially the women. Stead knew a great deal about men and their love for farm machinery but he demonstrates little or no knowledge of the human heart. In the throes of mastering his straw-burner, Gander shouts, "This was life." My point will be that this is patently not life, that what Stead too often writes about is at the periphery of what life and the novel are all about.

Stead's mechanistic views on human life are typical of a widespread school of thought visible in North American fiction

since the turn of the century. One of its spokesmen is Professor
Roy Meyer, the American writer and critic. He "repeatedly
stresses the primary significance of farm fiction as social com-
mentary rather than artistic creation" (5). His recipe for a good
farm novel is one that handles well the physical details of
farming, uses the vernacular in an authentic way, and reflects
and accepts attitudes characteristic of farm folk. These are rural
conservatism, anti-intellectualism, and hostility to the "town."
"Authentic farm fiction," he continues, "the product of writers
whose knowledge of rural life is sound and extensive, will
reproduce with great fidelity the daily and seasonal tasks of the
farmer and his family, their amusements and social activities,
and the sights, sounds, and smells of the physical environment
in which they live" (8). But how are we to know when we are
reading the farm fiction of an "authentic" artist? Authentic artists
are easy for Meyer to locate: "In general, one may assume that
the more details an author uses, the more he knows about the
kind of farm life he is describing, and the fewer details, the less
he knows" (8). It is not surprising, from this manifesto, that
Meyer avoids mentioning Faulkner and Steinbeck in his study
of American farm novels. If alert readers are going to discuss,
teach, or espouse the cause of our national literature as literature,
we must treat it as an art, and as such read it critically, not simply
as data for sociological inferences, as Mr. Meyer does.

Frederick Philip Grove is very often regarded as Canada's first
great "serious" novelist of the twentieth century. Not only has
Meyer lauded Grove's work, but the late Desmond Pacey wrote
the following tribute in 1961: "The greatest type of novel, which
seeks to penetrate deeply into the consciousness of its characters,
into the nature of a society or into the constitution of the
universe, was not practised at all in Canada prior to the
emergence of F.P. Grove in 1925, and even since that time it has
appeared only intermittently and imperfectly" (269). Curiously,
he cites the "sustained power" of *Fruits of the Earth* (1933) as an
example of this "greatest type of novel." Yet in spite of some
honest attempts to engage the subject of man and woman in an
unsentimental fashion, Grove is often as guilty as Stead and his

contemporaries of avoiding the business of characterization, especially of women. A good example of this failure is in *Fruits of the Earth*, often praised somewhat thoughtlessly for its novelistic qualities. Its protagonists are Abe and Ruth Spalding, homesteaders in Manitoba from Ontario.

Here is a descriptive passage typical of Grove in its photographic selection of materials for our viewing. Ruth has been looking at the latest installations in the great house Abe has just built. The fixtures have just been described with great energy and technical knowledge.

> Ruth betrayed no interest. Yet, with the warmer weather, she changed for the first time in years to light-coloured clothing. Not all of her new things were to Abe's taste; nor did they all fit well; but she had made an attempt, and he gave her credit for it. He went further. One day he returned from Somerville with a parasol of pearl-grey silk; she stared as she thanked him; the thought of the money it had cost appalled her; yet he had thought of her while in town. He promptly bought her a fur coat, a grey Siberian squirrel. (115)

I called this passage photographic, meaning merely photographic. Like most of Grove's descriptive passages in this novel, the emphasis is on externals: Ruth is mute but her clothes announce themselves in terms of colour, cut, style, and especially, cost. We are told a great deal about her coat but we are given no explanation as to why Ruth "betrayed no interest" in the fixtures of her new house. Nor are any of her new clothes mentioned again, so they are not allowed to accrue any symbolic value. The value of this description seems to lie scarcely deeper than the surface. Its connotative range is severely limited. Here is another look at Ruth in the latter half of the novel:

> When she scanned herself in a mirror—as a rule she used it only as an indispensable means of putting hairpins and clothes in the approximately right places—she felt amazed at the change she had undergone in the last twenty years. Her massive jaw sprang forward from a triple chin; the skin of her neck was heavily corrugated. The line from her shoulderblades sloped forward to

the top of her head. On her back, the flesh bulged as much as on her bosom. In walking, she balanced her weight on one foot before she lifted the other. It was tragic that this mockery of the human form should yet be the seat of poignant emotions. (150)

The details of the passage are selected as if Abe, her husband, chose them. The selection is made by a man who "had been in love with a face and a figure rather than a mind or soul." The details as they are arranged do not bespeak a strong empathy for the woman they describe. Our access to the things that define her character is impeded by our focus upon how fat she has grown. We have almost no access to her faded dreams, her fantasies, her memories, the quality of her consciousness, her specific emotional make-up. The narrator is viewing Ruth through the limited perceptions of his very limited protagonist. Later on we'll see that the narrator sermonizes remarkably like Abe himself.

It is characteristic of Grove's method that he spends almost all of his imaginative energy on the external evidence of these "poignant emotions" rather than attempting to render such emotions internally. For instance, his narrator comments on Ruth's widening girth at least six times in the latter part of the novel but scarcely ever alludes to her dreams or her past or the motives behind her (usually unspecified) poignant emotions. When we are finally allowed to eavesdrop on Ruth, the book is nearly over. When this does occur, the development proceeds almost entirely by means of dialogues, but Ruth's diction is inert and artificial.

We do not get to know Ruth. We are allowed to see Abe from many vantage points in the narration, but we are only allowed to see Ruth through severely insensitive eyes. This novel abounds in descriptions like the ones I have quoted. They typify Grove's fascination with details that direct our attention away from an engagement with his characters and toward an appraisal of the novel's physical surroundings or the characters' material endowments. If this sort of narrative focus seems tedious, perhaps it is because we are assuming the wrong things about it. So far the assumption has been that *Fruits of the Earth* is a novel. Yet even M.G. Parks, who lauds this book with the most enthusiastic of Grove critics, is forced to speak apologetically about Grove's inert sense of characterization in *Fruits of the Earth*. "His penetration into the human personality is seldom deep, and the reason is . . . that Grove's rather cold self-centredness severely limited his sympathetic understanding of other people, real or fictional" (xii). This is a fair judgement, but a puzzling thing to say about a realistic novel or the maker of one. There is scarcely a theorist since E.M. Forster who has not claimed that the realistic novel, as a serious fictional form, is committed to a thorough rendering of character. Like most postwar modernists, W.J. Harvey in his book *Character and the Novel* (1965) states that "most great novels exist to reveal and explore character" (23). Much of Grove's narrative functions as a kind of historical inventory of Spalding district. It photographs and documents the exterior of things and people. Their possessions are more important to Grove than their inner lives.

In apparent contradiction to the glowing claims of many critics of the book, Grove himself described it as follows: "*Fruits of the Earth* . . . was never intended to figure as a novel. I meant it to be taken as a piece of pioneer history" (Introduction to *Fruits*, viii). The title of the original manuscript was *Chronicles of Spalding District*, and by far Grove's preference of titles. Critics of this novel have tended to ignore this statement. The term "chronicles" is committed neither to realist novel conventions (such as depth of character portrayals or the presentation of manners), nor to the classical literary demands of an epic, which *Fruits* has also been called. A chronicle is an extended account of national or worldwide events over a considerable period of time in which no attempt is made by the chronicler to distinguish between fact and legend. Since Grove's book is not national or worldwide in scope, I have chosen to call it a regional chronicle, and not in any realist tradition but in a naturalistic tradition. These *Chronicles of Spalding District*, to use Grove's title, are a good example of what Northrop Frye calls "documentary naturalism":

> Literature deeply influenced by the descriptive aspect of symbolism is likely to tend toward the realistic in its narrative and toward the didactic or descriptive in its meaning. Its prevailing rhythm will be the prose of direct speech, and its main effort will be to give as clear and honest an impression of external reality as is possible with a hypothetical structure. In the documentary naturalism generally associated with such names as Zola and Dreiser, literature goes about as far as a representation of life, to be judged by its accuracy of description rather than by its integrity as a structure of words, as it could go and still remain literature. Beyond this point, the hypothetical or fictional element in literature would begin to dissolve. (79-80)

This brings us to one of the limitations of this book and perhaps of documentary naturalism in general. Frye notes "that the great age of documentary naturalism [was] the nineteenth century" (80). One reason for this is that in the twentieth century we have photographic and film documentaries to do, with much greater facility, what Grove is usually trying to do in his chronicle. There is scarcely a chapter in Grove's book in which he does not attempt to photograph his machinery, his school buildings, his characters' clothing, his school act, his brother-in-law's store, or Ruth's kitchen. One wearies of Abe's year-end financial reports, the size of his water pool, the style and condition of his fences. These countless inventories of equipment are of some interest to the archivist or the farm historian, but from a literary standpoint they have practically no dramatic or connotative function. They do not carry us beyond a materialistic concern for Abe's property. One would do well to remember the great *romans du terroir* of Grove's time: How D. H. Lawrence in *The Rainbow* works with such commonplace items as church steeples, barns, and sheaves of oats so as to impart a resonantly symbolic value to these objects; how William Faulkner in *The Hamlet* works just as effectively with such everyday objects as a snap-on bow tie, a plug of chewing tobacco, or a cow.

I suggested earlier that Grove's observations of Ruth, insensitive as they are to her inner nature, to the quality of her consciousness, seem very close to the observations Abe Spalding would choose to make of his wife. And in case it was ever in doubt that Grove and Spalding were of the same mind regarding their patriarchal point of view, watch as Grove steps out of the action momentarily to instruct us on the evils of modern democracy, the Jazz Age, and Eros:

> The war had unsettled men's minds. There was a tremendous new urge toward immediacy of results . . . Irrespective of their economic ability, people craved things which they had never craved before. Democracy was interpreted as the right of every-body to everything that the stimulated inventive power of mankind in the mass could furnish in the way of conveniences and luxuries. Amusements became a necessity of daily life. A tendency to spend recklessly and to use credit on a scale hitherto unknown was linked with a pronounced weakening of the moral fibre. In the homes . . . gramophones and similar knick-knacks made their appearance; young men wore flashy clothes, paying or owing from forty to a hundred dollars for a suit. Girls wore silk stockings, silk underwear, silk dresses; and nothing destroys modesty and sexual morality in a girl more quickly than the consciousness that suddenly she wears attractive dessous. (223)

The point of view in the above passage may fairly be described as patriarchal, an expression of Logos alienated from the life-affirming wisdom of Eros. Let us now turn to Martha Ostenso's *Wild Geese* (1925), and see how a remarkably similar storyline can be fleshed out in such a way as to present the characters with greater depth and richness.

In terms of the mere plot, *Wild Geese* is remarkably similar to Grove's *Fruits of the Earth*. Both novels were set in rural Manitoba. Both stories concluded *circa* 1920. Both authors, to a significant extent, focus on the domestic scene of families that in both cases are presided over by rigidly puritanical patriarchs: Abe Spalding of *Fruits of the Earth* and Caleb Gare of *Wild Geese*. Both patriarchs have submissive wives who both bear four children, two sons and two daughters. Both patriarchs favour and spoil one of their sons, and in both cases that son's name is Charlie. In both books one of the daughters rebels and becomes pregnant out of wedlock: in Grove's book, Frances

Spalding; in Ostenso's, Judith Gare. Both patriarchs, as they grow older, come to value their crops, their homesteads, and generally their material possessions to the near exclusion of their familial affections, especially the love of their wives. Both patriarchs are resented by the less successful homesteaders in the district, and in both books, these material ambitions are the undoing of the two patriarchs.

One would almost be tempted to say that Grove published his book eight years later as an answer to Ostenso's. I know. I'm speculating. But let's keep these remarkable similarities in mind. I will be coming back to them.

In spite of these similarities, *Fruits of the Earth* and *Wild Geese* are emphatically dissimilar books. One of the ways in which the vast difference between the books can be discussed is in terms of the contrasting values imbedded in these plots. The modern forces that permeated Spalding District are corrupt and ruinous. They represent the prosperous and unrestrained morality of the roaring twenties. The country dance hall becomes a gathering place for corruption. But in *Wild Geese* Lind Archer's urban values, her dance music, her silken "dessous," her education, are liberating forces. Patriarchal values similar to those of Abe Spalding, when proclaimed by Caleb Gare in *Wild Geese*, are villainized. Matriarchal forces operate to undermine Caleb Gare's iron hold on his family. Let us meet some of Martha Ostenso's women and the man who tyrannizes them. Here is Caleb's wife Amelia in her kitchen area. This sketch contrasts interestingly with Grove's "photographs" of Ruth Spalding:

> Amelia came and stood by the table. She turned up the wick of the lamp slightly. As she did so, the light picked out the shadows under her eyes, the rigid lines about her mouth, the pale sandy hair whitening about her temples. Amelia was fifty and was beginning to put on flesh, but she bore herself with a dignified reserve that seemed almost a part of her physical being, so that the grace which was hers in youth still clung to her. She seemed preposterously ill-fitted to her environment. Lind was filled with pity as she watched her move about the room, picking up a paper, straightening a doily or, from a habit Lind realized must

have been formed in another life, pulling down the shades before the windows. (16)

The sketch begins with the same kind of photographic details we recall in sketches of Ruth's faded beauty, but it terminates with a departure from physical detail so that Amelia's features may be analysed. They are presented through the sympathetic witnessing consciousness of Lind Archer who notes her reserve, her grace, and the incongruity of her presence in this rude environment. Whether or not Grove contrives it, we are often urged to view Ruth negatively because she becomes fat or looks dowdy. This is because Grove's third person narrator usually voices the insensitive attitudes of Abe Spalding. Both men seem to feel it "tragic that this mockery of a human form [Ruth's] should be the seat of poignant emotions." But in Ostenso's passage we are allowed to sympathize with the oppressed prairie wife. The point of view is decidedly matriarchal.

When the sympathies of a story develop from an archetypally feminine point of view, and when that point of view eventually *dominates* views antagonistic to it, then a story's slant can be said to be matriarchal. The archetypal feminine sensibility, whether in this book or in literature generally, is in tune with the laws of nature, in tune with the earthy wisdom of Eros. In this love for the earth, Eros contrasts with Logos, which just as often attempts to conquer the earth. The above sketch is not merely more sympathetic toward womankind. After all, in his autobiographical novel *Search for America*, Grove claimed his "sympathies were with the women." Ostenso's sketch is empathetic. It goes beyond the snapshot, into the gestures, and beyond the gestures of the prairie wife into her private self. We watch her as she tidies up the stark room fastidiously. When we see the incongruity of these actions we can understand the reasons for her lack of fulfilment from a point of view close to her own. And this empathetic rendering of character may be seen in Ostenso's other women as well.

Let us examine, for instance, Ostenso's most assertive and dynamic female creation, Judith Gare, daughter of Caleb and Amelia: "She had a great, defiant body, her chest high and broad as a boy's; her hair was wild-locked and black and shone on top of her head with a bluish luster; her eyes were in sullen repose now, long and narrow; her lips were rich and drooped at the corner. She wore overalls and a heavy sweater, and stood squarely on her feet, as if prepared to take or give a blow" (11).

In a later scene, Judith is looking at Caleb's bull calves. It is interesting to note, again, how the narrative begins in photographic details but terminates in an evaluation of these details. The sketch ultimately focuses attention back on the witnessing sensibility of Judith.

> She leaned against the fence and looked in at two of the plump young bulls who were dancing about playfully skulling each other, having apparently just discovered their sprouting horns. She saw how they had developed since she had last observed them. Their grizzled, stupid faces had become more surly, their flanks heavier, their dewlaps smoother and whiter and thicker. Caleb would soon be ringing their noses, and they would become spiritlessly ugly, with all this madcap frenzy suppressed. They were beautiful bulls, and would bring a nice sum from one of the Icelanders, perhaps. Judith felt an inner excitement in watching them. She turned to go, feeling dismayed that she should be so attracted by the young beasts. But a curiosity over which she had no control held her there for many minutes. Ah, how violent they were becoming in their play. (54)

This sketch is more than a snapshot, much more than the inventory one associates with the documentary naturalism of Grove. The bulls provide a projection of Judith's amazonian sexuality. The bulls' burgeoning sexuality and their frenzied love of combat provide a foreshadowing of Judith's combat for mastery over her lover, Sven Sandbo, later in the novel. As the lovers wrestle in the dust they are "two stark elements, striving for mastery over each other" (86). Because the bulls' madcap frenzy strikes a responsive note in Judith's unconscious, she is dismayed that Caleb would soon be suppressing what is natural in them.

In the case of the patriarchs, Abe and Caleb, this suppression of natural desire is necessary to keep the family working on the farm. Sexuality is a major threat. Regarding his older daughter, Abe says, "Satisfy sexual instincts at that stage, and higher things cease" (195). And when he hears a rumour that his younger daughter is not a virgin, Abe wishes her dead. But where Grove tries to incorporate Abe's neurosis for control and suppression into a heroic defence of the old morality, Ostenso singles out this neurosis for rhetorical attack.

In the above sketch of Judith and the bulls, one is able to see into the deep-seated antagonism between Judith and her father. It is so primitive it is almost subverbal. Yet it is rendered quite resonantly in this and similar sketches. A rendering of such antagonism is not possible in the Grove story because the limitations of his photographic style are too severe. This merely underlines why Grove wanted to call his book a chronicle. In a chronicle he is relieved of some of the responsibility of breathing life into his cardboard women, Ruth, Frances, and Marion. Even the women who submit to relatively traditional sex roles in *Wild Geese* (Ellen, Amelia, and Lind Archer) have a lifelike quality to them. Ellen is the oldest daughter of Caleb and, unlike Judith, totally intimidated and enslaved by him. Notice how in this passage, while Grove might have been more interested in the cost and colour of her clothing and her physical size, Ostenso goes beyond the typical Grove inventory. Her modifying words participate to some extent in the agony of Ellen's enslavement.

> While Judith helped in the kitchen, Ellen obediently went to the organ. She sat erect and prim in her washed-out gingham dress, that had apparently shrunk and grown too small even for her narrow shoulders and uncertain breast. Her fine brown hair, that was lighter in colour and much less luxuriant than Judith's, was drawn back without a relenting wave from her rather prominent, austerely white brow. Her eyebrows were exquisitely shaped and black as ink-lines. Behind the magnifying glass of her spectacles her dark blue eyes swam liquid and vague. Her raw-looking, thin fingers sought out the keys. (15)

Grove seems aware of some of Spalding's emotional deficiencies; that, for instance, he "had been in love with a face and a figure rather than mind or soul." But in *Fruits* Grove can hardly claim to be much more perceptive than Abe, or indeed value Abe's three women for much more than their bodies and how they dress them. It hardly comes as a surprise when Abe wishes his deflowered daughter dead or that he never is reconciled with her by the end of the book. Caleb Gare, too, is emotionally impoverished. But his impoverishment becomes a rich resource for Ostenso to dramatize. Here, for instance, is Caleb in his beloved field of flax, which he loves primarily for its economic potential:

> While he was raptly considering the tender field of flax—now in blue flower—Amelia did not exist to him. There was a transcendent power in this blue field of flax that lifted a man above the petty artifices of birth, life, and death. It was more exacting, even than an invisible God. It demanded not only the good in him, but the evil, and the indifference. Caleb would stand for long moments outside the fence beside the flax. Then he would turn quickly to see that no one was looking. He would creep between the wires and run his hand across the flowering, gentle tops of the growth. A stealthy caress—more intimate than any he had ever given to woman. (119)

The eroticism of this passage is explicit enough to reduce Caleb's petty ambitions to the level of perverted desire. Caleb is twisted and gnarled and stunted, harsh and demanding like the land he assails. His head and shoulders "loomed forward from the rest of his body like a rough projection of rock" (113), but the lower half of his body visibly dwindled. His physical appearance suggests harshness and sterility, and this of course tallies with his emotional and spiritual life.

I have said that Ostenso's story proceeds from a basically matriarchal position, with all the earthy, life-affirming values that this position implies. In *Wild Geese* there is an interesting delineation between characters who conquer or defy the earth and those who wish to live in harmony with it. Parallel to Caleb's exploitation of Amelia and his family, and his ultimate failure to reduce them all to servility, is Caleb's relation to the earth. He mines the soil to capitalize on his flax crop. In the end it has its vengeance on him, quite literally sucking him into its "overstrong embrace" (237). When Judith is alone and unencumbered by work, she loves the soil and recognizes in it perhaps the same living force that kills Caleb. At one point, for example, she strips in the woods and lies naked on the earth, thinking, "Oh, how knowing the bare earth was, as if it might have a heart and a mind hidden here in the woods. The fields that Caleb had tilled had no tenderness, she knew. But here was something forbiddenly beautiful, secret as one's own body" (53). In this delineation of attitudes to the land there could not be a more strikingly dramatized juxtaposition of Logos in conflict with Eros. And Eros, of course, as it is embodied by Amelia, Lind, and Judith, is exalted much above the futile machinations of Caleb, the most extreme example of Logos in the book. The matriarchal forces endure and prevail. This is not to imply that the women prevail, or even that the women are the sole embodiments of Eros. Eros is, after all, an intuitive wisdom that generates its mysterious and fecund powers in harmony with nature. It is wisdom often associated with women, but wisdom accessible to both sexes, as is Logos.

A good example of the primacy of the wisdom of Eros can be seen in two deliberately juxtaposed sections in *Wild Geese*. In the first section Caleb reads the Bible to his family, deriding the man who "eateth his own flesh" and "is alone when he falleth" (41-42). It is a reminder for the family to cleave together under the tyrannical thumb of Caleb himself. The power of his sermon does not come through the scriptures but through the irony they generate in Caleb's voice. For the fool Caleb describes so piously in his sermon is himself. He preaches a wisdom he neither believes nor understands. Then the novel moves right to the second section and the home and family of Erik Bjarnasson and his wife, the blind fortuneteller who spins. The old lady tells Lind's fortune, predicting that soon she will have a lover: "You will never know the secret of him. But you will be happy" (45). This is, of course, exactly what happens to Lind soon after. The day ends with Mathias Bjarnasson telling them old tales:

He had lived much in common with solitude, and had come to know that there is an unmeasurable Alone surrounding each soul, and that nameless and undreamed are the forms that drift within that region. So that it was well for the members of a great family to cleave together and so ward off the menaces and the dreads of the great Alone. When the Teacher went to bed finally, the storm had abated. High above the soughing of the wind under the great eaves of the stone house, Lind heard the trailing clangour of the wild geese. Their cry smote upon the heart like the loneliness of the universe . . . a magnificent seeking through solitude—an endless quest. (46-47)

The geese affirm what the old lady and Mathias have spoken about. The geese bespeak an intuitive primitive wisdom. They symbolize the lonely quest and the need for love. And it is the Bjarnassons who truly cleave together. What they live each day is the intuitive wisdom of Eros, the feminine wisdom that is the driving force behind this book's rhetoric.

Wild Geese is by no means a flawless book in terms of its presentation of characters. Mark Jordan, the book's hero, is introduced to the settlement by rather artificial means. His diction is badly stilted and his love affair with Lind Archer is as vapid as romance can get. At times the lovers become unforgivably condescending toward the rural characters. As well, there is such a clear delineation between the evil and good characters (between Caleb and the women, in other words), that Ostenso's point of view obtrudes into the life of her characters. She is most convincing in her creations of women in defiance of men (Judith) or men oppressing women (Caleb). That is to say, she comes down heavily in the defence of Eros in combat with Logos. She is decidedly less successful in her attempt to marry these forces, as witness the stiffly formalized and stylized affair between Mark and Lind.

As I stated before, roughly the same story has been told first from a matriarchal point of view (Ostenso's), then from a patriarchal point of view (Grove's). The details of the two plots are *so* similar, I long suspected that Grove's book was written as a sort of patriarchal rebuke to Ostenso. Imagine my delight when I discovered this letter written by Grove in 1925 to a friend, the year Ostenso's prizewinning novel was published. Here is Grove's opinion of *Wild Geese*:

> The book is deplorably, even unusually immature . . . There is a teacher, Miss Ostenso, drawn by stencil, pretty, charming, etc., with all the conventional reactions of the NEW WOMAN which exist only in books. There is Mark Jordan, the . . . dream of every 'tame goose' . . . There is the oppressed mother and wife with a past, held in submission by an impossible threat. Only in books is such a threat effective: in life it does not work. There is also a . . . rebellious daughter: what could be more stencil work than that rebellion? . . . Not one of them all is more than a drawing; not one of them lives. Now all this is, of course, only natural when an immature young girl sits down to write a book, not because that book cries in her to be written; but because she has the itch to write. She knows nothing of the grim things of life . . . One character is seen, in glimpses; Caleb Gare. He is not understood . . . no attempt is made to understand him. The book is written as a prosecutor's plea against him to ensure conviction. Whenever he acts, he forgets who he is . . . A man like that does not by mistake run into a slough which he knows. That end, untrue and silly, destroys the one tragic possibility of the book . . . in order to understand [Caleb Gare] we must see his side of the case . . . Needless to say, the book is reasonably well written . . . The petty 'sexiness' of many passages makes a mature person smile . . . In fact, how could a young girl know anything of the fierce antagonisms that discharge themselves in sex? . . . It's the old story: only trash wins a prize . . .
> *(Letters of Frederick Philip Grove, 25-26)*

It seems clear to me that Grove wrote *Fruits* in part as an attempt to retell Ostenso's "immature" story from Caleb's "side of the case." This is the only way I can explain the many startling similarities between the plots (listed above). As fiction, Ostenso's book is more effective, perhaps in spite of the fact that her male protagonists are either somewhat stiff creations (Mark) or as villainous as characters in romance can be (Caleb). In contrast, Grove's women are the ones who elicit our contempt, either as human beings or as fictive structures. Our interest in character denied us, we must turn our attention toward Grove's countless inventories and descriptions of prairie farming. And these details bind Grove's chronicle to its time and place, preventing its leap into universality. *Fruits of the Earth* is therefore a regional work in the most confining sense of that word.

One might wonder if any writer at this time could produce a story that was both faithful to the essential character of this region and that achieved a certain measure of universal significance. And one might also wonder if a balance was ever struck between the matriarchal and patriarchal points of view in the fiction of this time. The answer to both these questions is, Yes: *La Forêt* by Georges Bugnet (1935).

The balance between Eros and Logos, it must be remembered, is a balance between two opposite psychic dispositions: one which pursues a conquest over the natural order and one which seeks a harmony with it. In novelistic terms this balance implies that both sides are allowed equal time for debate, so to speak. And neither side is reduced to the level of a villainous tyrant (which we see so often in romance fiction) or an inert blob like Ruth Spalding. In Canadian prairie fiction one sees an overwhelming number of cases in which the allegiance rests too exclusively with masculine or with feminine forces to give a balanced picture of man and woman. The story is usually something like this: The patriarch's law is the law of the household. The patriarch's work is sacred, and it enslaves the prairie wife and her family as well. This work is such that it assaults nature in a violent conquest. The Logos mentality has free rein and Eros is strangled into submission or forced to rebel. Bugnet's protagonist, Roger Bourgouin, is a strong representative of the Logos principle, which actively suppresses the wisdom of Eros. Originally he was a scholarly young writer from France who came to the West with his sophisticated young wife, Louise. He farms like a conqueror doing battle. He assaults the forest with his axe, and when his progress is too slow to make a profit, he hires two labourers to help him. His idea is to make a killing in five or so years and return to France a veritable seigneur. He is sure he can augment their meagre income by his writing in the winters. Soon after he and his wife arrive in the forest to homestead, Roger's farming becomes his sole obsession. But when winter comes and his external labours all but cease, the creative wellsprings are dry. He cannot write, for he has denied the imaginative side of his nature. His battle with the forest is consuming his soul.

Much of the narrative concerning Roger's decline is filtered through the perceptions of his wife. In this way *La Forêt* is perhaps even more Louise's story than Roger's. It is Louise who properly sees the danger in Roger's decline from a sensitive, loving intellectual with great dreams, to an obsessed, emotionally dry and tired man. It is Louise who foretells the disaster that eventually overtakes them at the hands of the indomitable forest. It is Louise who maintains a consistent relationship with the numinous realities evoked like primitive gods from the heart of the forest. She is the very personification of Eros, and therefore, because her husband has forced them into the role of nature's enemy, she fears she is being forced to betray the forest. It begins to frighten her. The only point in the novel when she feels at one with the forest is after she has given birth to her first child, and she can somehow identify with the life-giving functions of the earth. At this point Bugnet modulates his often grim tone to one of ecstasy. This numinous response to the dark mysterious forces of creation is emotional and instinctual, not rational. It bespeaks a mystic sensibility capable of true awe, terror, ecstasy in the presence of the deity. Louise feels this but Roger has lost his capacity for such a response.

Bugnet's subject is the impact of the wilderness on the Bourgouins' marriage. Part of the strength of this book as a work of fiction is that Bugnet, like Sinclair Ross in As *For Me and My House*, confronts the subject of the marriage head-on. He does not merely photograph its outward trappings as Grove so often does in his fiction. He does not create villains and heroes as Ostenso does. He does not sentimentalize the despair of his heroine as Arthur Stringer does. And unlike Stead or Grove, he insists on exploring the woman's side of the story. Like Ross's Mrs. Bentley, Louise Bourgouin has a conventionally submissive manner, but is no less vibrantly alive for being submissive. The following passage is a rendering of much of what I have summarized above:

> Slowly, relentlessly, the wind augmented its violence, keeping them imprisoned. Through an opening melted in the hoarfrost on the window pane, she looked out at the pale grey sky. The invisible sun left a vague halo in the south, barely above the horizon. Sometimes this glimmer even disappeared completely, covered by immense flights of snow exploded out by the storm on the surface of the lake and hurled right toward the cabin. Desolation would whisper into Louise and then recede, whisper then recede, rise and fall. She imagined that the tempest sought to shroud them under a thick windingsheet, as if their tomb was already marked, here, at the edge of this forest. She sensed the forest's closeness, looming behind the wind. And from it too, she could hear similar sad clamourings in dreadful response to the formidable singing of the wind.
>
> Roger had to go out to tend the animals. When he came back, he broke out in resentment against the tempest:
>
> "Goddam weather! All I did was go to the creek and chop a drinking hole for the animals, and look at me. Frozen solid. Aiyaiyai . . . Oh, well. The wind does some good. It's cleaned out all the snow banked up around the cabin and swept all the snow off the top of the hill. I guess it all piles up in the woods" (88-89).

Note how the storm outside precipitates the emergence of the two peoples' awareness. Note how the quality of their awareness differs: the introspective, instinctual, quasi-superstitious dread of Louise; the externalized belligerence of Roger. And note how through Louise's fearful reveries and Roger's truculent, taciturn remarks we are allowed to participate with empathy in the incompatibility of the two alienated lovers. The book dramatizes humanity's minuteness away from the insularity of society and in the presence of omnipotent nature. The way to mitigate this sense of minuteness, this cosmic loneliness, lies less through scientific farming and brute strength than through love. Logos must be joined with Eros. Logos must learn from Eros or they both will perish.

I began by questioning not Grove's sagacity so much as that of Grove's entourage of eulogizers. One of their claims was for the so-called novelistic qualities of *Fruits of the Earth*, a chronicle that does not truly aspire to the definition of a realist novel because it avoids characterization in favour of the external realities of Spalding District. It is regional in a confining sense, directing our attention toward details that do not particularly enrich his story. Now watch how Bugnet, with a similar storyline in a similar region, directs our attention toward a wider vision of things, transcending the regional bounds of time and place into something much more universal. The following passage is seen through Louise's fearful, sensitive eyes:

> There was no wind and the air was cold, penetrating everything with a tranquil intensity. The night sky was serenely pure. Stars like silver flakes of nevermelting snow remained motionless in their permanent pattern of nocturnal circling. The big lake slept its peaceful sleep. To the north, silent and undisturbed, was the dark outline of the forest, its advance guard of towering giants brooding over uncountable millions, guarding the vast, ancient country that it covered with its powerful and varied multitudes of vegetable civilization, stretching all the way to the barren lands where even trees cannot live. And Louise sensed also that from the spot where she was standing, these robust protectors of the soil were massing their armies, nearly everywhere, along the great rivers of the north and far up to the polar seas bordering Canada. In the calm face of that cold, as relentless as it was devoid of hate, before that immense enigmatic firmament, that enormous forest which had made her a prisoner here, Louise felt a rising fear and despair. So weak, so defenceless, facing those powers at once formidable and peaceful, she shuddered as she felt the ranging emptiness. Why try to struggle against that calm and occult grandeur to which man and his works are nothing but fleeting and imperceptible atoms, swarming for an instant like animated dust—then reabsorbed, they and their works, under the epidermis of a minute globe that before and after

them, follows its own destiny along an unknown road lost in unfathomable space?

Recoiling from this sense of nothingness and from the cold, the shadows on the snow, the solitude and the silence, she cried out desperately: "Roger! . . . Roger! . . ."

And then she saw him, a dark moonshadow on the snow, approaching her. She ran to him. (97-98)

In the first paragraph of the above quotation Bugnet widens his focus from the lake, the woods, the immediate surroundings beneath the stars to include the whole wheeling universe. Louise's particular anxiety becomes the existential terror of all humankind "swarming for an instant like animated dust" on a minute globe. In moments like this a prairie novel ceases to be regional and speaks poignantly to other people in other lands about loneliness and the need for love.

In the first third of this century our novelists reduced their female personages to mere shadows of women. No wonder the Martha Ostensos of the world rose like avenging Amazons to the aid of their sisters to take revenge on the prairie patriarch or any patriarch whose eyes were closed to the women around them.

References

Bugnet, Georges. 1976. *The Forest.* Montreal: Harvest House. First published in 1935.

Faulkner, William. 1949. "Nobel Prize Acceptance Speech." Stockholm, 1949.

Frye, Northrop. 1957. *Anatomy of Criticism.* Princeton: Princeton University Press.

Grove, F.P. 1965. *Fruits of the Earth.* Toronto: McClelland and Stewart (NCL), with an Introduction by M.G. Parks. First published in 1933.

Grove, F.P. 1976. *Letters of F.P. Grove.* Edited by Desmond Pacey Toronto: University of Toronto Press.

Harding, M. Esther. 1971, 1990. *Woman's Mysteries: Ancient and Modern.* Longmans, 1935. Reprint, Boston and New York: Shambhala.

Harvey, W.J. 1965. *Character and the Novel.* London: Chatto and Windus.

Lawrence, D.H. 1967. *Phoenix.* London: William Heinemann.

Meyer, Roy. 1965. *The Middle Western Farm Novel in the Twentieth Century.* Lincoln: University of Nebraska Press.

Ostenso, Martha. 1971. *Wild Geese.* Toronto: McClelland and Stewart (NCL). First published in 1925.

Pacey, Desmond. 1961. *Creative Writing in Canada.* Toronto: Ryerson.

Smith, A.J.M. 1954. *Our Sense of Identity.* Edited by Malcolm Ross. Toronto: Ryerson.

Stead, R.J.C. 1966. *Grain.* Toronto: McClelland and Stewart (NCL). First published in 1926.

Stead, R.J.C. 1924. *The Smoking Flax.* Toronto: McClelland and Stewart.

Nomme de Plume

GEORGES BUGNET (NOVELIST, SCIENTIST, POET, SETTLER)
was born in France in 1879, the same year as Frederick Philip
Grove. When I was in graduate school I found some biographical
sketches of him, but nowhere could I find a date for his death.
Grove (alias Felix Paul Berthold Friederich Greve), the son of a
minor official in Hamburg, reinvented himself as an aristocratic
Anglo-Swede. He fooled everyone about his true identity until
decades after his death. But at least he left us with a corpse, a
gravesite. Bugnet's coup seemed to be that he was immortal. In
1971 or so, it didn't occur to me that he might still be alive.

Here is what the eminent critic E.K. Brown said in 1947 about
La Forêt, Bugnet's masterpiece:

> Last week I was asked . . . what was the finest novel of the
> Canadian West. I . . . thought of two . . . novels, Frederick Philip
> Grove's *Settlers of the Marsh* and Sinclair Ross's *As For Me and
> My House*. But the book I actually name gives . . . a deeper
> sounding of life in the West than either of these . . . The book is
> . . . Georges Bugnet's *La Forêt* . . . Bugnet . . . is one of the really
> important Canadian writers. In him an intellect and spirit of a
> very high order unite with a long experience of life in the
> wilderness; and the result has been a literary work in which the
> materials of the frontier have been wrought into designs of lasting
> beauty, and their meaning presented with an unwavering courage
> . . . It is a great and tragic book. We do not have many such.

I discovered *La Forêt* (1935) in 1971. I was a grad student writing
a doctoral thesis in Edmonton. My supervisor was Mort Ross,

an American literature specialist who was on a sabbatical during the time I was reading Bugnet. With Mort gone, the job fell to Dick Harrison, a Canadian specialist. When Harrison was away on research, my supervisor was Rudy Wiebe. Even then, Rudy was a writer of some repute and he noticed things about my thesis that writers would notice and scholars might not. Dick Harrison was just discovering material about settlement narratives that he would eventually write a great deal about. He would set me straight on matters bearing on Canadian literature and history. Mort Ross had an osprey's unfaltering eye for sloppy prose, jargon-hazed thinking, and evasive arguments. So with Mort and Dick and Rudy, I had the best of three worlds. For two years they shared me like foster parents.

La Forêt hit me very hard. My own French was pretty lame, but in time I improved and reread all of Bugnet's works. I fell beneath the spell of his voice and acquired a slavish anglo respect for French. How timid these anglo writers were on the subject of love. Love. You could say the word without moving your lips. But *amour*. Now there was a doozer of a word. Watch the mouths of the francophones. *Amour*.

How could a bland word like "dusk" stand up to *crépuscule?* Ah, zose English, zey ave no soul. How I longed to be French!

And how strange to do research on a man who apparently was immortal. I must have dreamed of meeting with Bugnet and talking with him about the Big Issues. Art, Politics, and Love. I began on weekends to drive to the French communities north of Edmonton to see if there was anyone who had known Georges Bugnet. I tried St. Albert and Morinville. My third stop was Legal, about an hour's drive north of Edmonton. I drove there through a snowstorm and parked my car at the old folks' home. An elderly Sister greeted me at the door.

I said something like the following to her: "Have you ever heard of a man named Bugnet?"

"We have a Bugnet here," she said in French.

"Georges Bugnet?"

"Yes," she said.

"Is he . . . all right?"

"He is very old," she said.

"Is this Georges Bugnet the writer?"

"I don't know if he writes anything," she said. "He *talks* a lot."

She showed me to his room, I knocked on the door, and a gravelly voice shouted, "*Entrez, entrez.*"

I walked into a small dim room with a bunk bed and a tiny desk. The room smelled strongly of pipe tobacco. A short man with a scraggly white beard was lying on the bed.

"Are you Georges Bugnet?" I said.

"Yes," he said.

"Georges Bugnet, the *writer?*"

It was the old man's turn to look incredulous. He sat up in his bunk. "You have read my books?" he said.

The next day I burst into Rudy Wiebe's office. It was heaped with photocopies of old newspapers. He was becoming steeped in Cree and Métis lore and the hateful propaganda in the Orange press of the 1870s and 1880s. He was writing his first draft of *The Temptations of Big Bear*. All through the winter he seemed to be visited by wave upon wave of furious inspiration. This was also one of those months when Rudy had been assigned to supervise my thesis. Alas, in 1971 he had bigger fish to fry.

"Georges Bugnet is alive!" I cried. "I've just spoken with him!"

"Hm," said Rudy. He managed to sound as though my discovery was the third or fourth most pressing thing on his mind. "That would mean that he's—what—ninety-three?"

"Something like that."

"So?"

"Oh, nothing. Just thought you might be interested."

"I am," he said, glancing at his watch.

My weekly trips out to Legal began as necessary scholarship. But soon Bugnet and I strayed off the scholarly topics and onto the Big Issues. On one such occasion, he told me that I should have a wife. His exact words were, "*C'est pas bon, l'homme sans épouse.*"

I still have these words on an old cassette from an interview I did with him for the *Journal of Canadian Fiction.* At the time he said this, he was well into his nineties, and I was twenty-nine. When I last came to visit him, he was 102 and still extolling the virtues of marriage in French and English. When I could still call myself a young man, Georges Bugnet came rather close, I suppose, to the human equivalent of God. He had that effect on the many people I brought out to meet him, even when he was lost and rambling.

"Carpenter, you should try for one in Beau Monde."

"Try for what?"

"Go to Beau Monde," he went on. "The last time I was there . . . beautiful French girls. You should go soon. They want husbands and they make lovely wives."

"Beau Monde?"

"*Oui.*"

Beautiful world. A world of perfect love. She and I walking naked in some garden, God speaking to us in a stately French accent.

"Where is Beau Monde?"

"You must have approached it sometime, going to or from Edmonton." In a dreamy voice he added, "I think by now it must be not so far."

Can you imagine how this news must have struck me in Bugnet's rasping voice? *Elles font de belles épouses.* I suspect Bugnet had not been anywhere in twenty years, let alone to Beau Monde, Alberta, wherever that was. So naturally I thought he was talking nonsense. But somewhere else, where bushes that burn become burning bushes, I thought, *God is trying to tell me something.* And how the phrase *belles épouses* plucked melodies on the strings of my heart. All the way back to Edmonton, I probably mumbled words like *beau monde* and *belles épouses* like a rosary. (To this day I dream about that ride home from Legal. It always involves a futile search for love and always leaves the same aching residue. I'm driving fast because I've missed a rendezvous. I awaken to the memory of a woman's voice.)

I drove back toward Edmonton beneath a darkening winter

sky, and I found myself thinking in a more familiar language. I am still young. I am only twenty-nine years old. I am not ready for six children and the paunch of a church elder even if some of my friends are. Until this time I had always opted for the woman with a sign over her head: THIS RELATIONSHIP WILL SELF-DESTRUCT IN SIXTY DAYS. A strange time in my life, if you see what I mean.

Somehow I managed to drive past my usual turnoff to the heart of Edmonton and instead drive south and east on an unfamiliar road. Along this road I spied the turnoff for Beaumont.

Of course, the village of Beaumont! I slowed, hesitated, trying to recall Bugnet's description of the old village. A gothic cathedral. Some old stone buildings, some statues of saints and virgins. But at the edge of the town, I saw none of these. Just row upon row of nearly identical pastel bungalows and duplexes on streets denuded of trees. Beaumont had become a bedroom community for commuters to Edmonton and looked determinedly Protestant to me. Protestant, perhaps even post-Christian.

I drove on, closer to the centre of town, past more bungalows, none of which might occasion a romantic utterance in French or in English. Past a flat pink school. But then a dip in the road, an old bridge, a slow-moving stream, and the last remnant of the old village square: a turn-of-the-century brick courthouse; facing it, an equally venerable stone cathedral; and a hotel so old in appearance, one would never mistake it for a motel. In this last little atoll of francophone culture, I parked my car.

Instinct led me to the coffee shop. Behind the counter was a rather plain waitress (no rings) speaking to an old man. The old man was stooped over a plate of French fries, which I suppose was appropriate, and the two of them were speaking, unmistakably, in French.

"*Un café, s'il vous plaît,*" I said. Perhaps teasingly.

All francophones in this part of the country speak English and recognize at once when an anglo is showing off his pathetic European textbook French. It's a game played by linguistic tourists: I will be French for you if you pretend that my French is acceptable.

"*Oui,*" she said. Not *wye* or *wa* as she might have said in a moment of low enthusiasm, but *oui.* She might just as well have said, *Je serai ta belle épouse.* Her *oui* had the same effect. Suddenly, with that one word, she was considerably less than plain.

All over English Canada when we WASPs affirm something, we say "yes." A terse syllable hissing from a mouth that moves almost grudgingly. This ultimate affirmation, this word that commands the blood to rush downward and release all of God's tumescence in a pledge of love. Yes? We move our lips so slightly that the word scarcely issues at all. This is not an affirmation. It is at best a furtive nod towards a workable compromise among people who want to keep their teeth warm and out of the wind.

But *oui.* My waitress purses her lips as if to whistle and they part in a burst that melts the snow and celebrates the whiteness of teeth and all the liquid wonder of her mouth. *Oui.* She cannot say this word without kissing the air between herself and me.

I was caught inside the plot of an old writer; I had become his young hero. I didn't wonder whether I'd forfeited my own language for someone else's or why my own value system seemed to have collapsed. I was taking cues from an unseen director, speaking my lines and hoping for a pleasant ending. It was clear in some unused part of my soul that God had sent me to this café—and that he wanted me married. As Bugnet would say, "You want in your body to be mated, and in your soul to be united to another."

My waitress brought a large cup of steaming black coffee and smiled. Her hair must have been quite long. It was black and glossy and gathered up in a fine roll with many errant wisps behind her ears. On her uniform blouse she had sewn the letters L-M.

"*Que veut dire ton monogramme?*" I asked. I pronounced her letters. Their sound came back to me like an echo: *elle aime, elle aime . . .*

"Louise Monpetit," she said.

"Dave Carpenter," I said.

"*Salut,* Dave."

The old man down the counter said something I didn't understand, and she returned to him. Louise Monpetit. (Note the *oui* in Louise.) No aspiring lovers hung around the counters. Perhaps all the men of the village had fled the onrush of pastel bungalows to make their fortune up north or in the city. Soon the last of the old town would fall to the anglo bulldozers. And what would happen to Louise Monpetit? The most preposterous scenario began to emerge. I saw my role clearly. I would marry her, join the Roman Catholic church, and become a champion of francophone culture in Beaumont. We would have two or three darkhaired sons and at least as many lovely daughters. They would speak perfect French , and they would repossess the town. I would become the town patriarch, coach the hockey team, and after I was gone, a statue of me in my coaching duds would stylite in front of the courthouse. I wondered whether Bugnet had ever considered such a plot.

I think I was glancing out the café window. The late afternoon gloom had imperceptibly turned to night. Winter. But the radiance of my scenario warmed me in my heart, and I realized that I could ask for nothing more. I turned to my waitress. Louise Monpetit, the last *belle épouse* in Beaumont, Alberta.

In English, she said, "Would you like anything more?"

As God is my witness, I faltered, looked down at my empty cup, and said, "No, thank you." And fled to my car.

There came a time, when my French had improved and I was finishing up my Ph.D., that I decided to translate *La Forêt* into English. This was the spring or summer of 1973. I approached Bugnet with the project. He said, "Your French could use some improvement, but most of all, you need to live in a forest."

"What?"

"You need to live in a forest. You need to watch what happens to the flora, what happens to the *saules*. You have been too long in the city, and my book is about a forest."

Right then and there I promised Bugnet that I would find a cabin in a forest and do his book. He agreed and we shook on it. I was awarded a post-doc at the University of Manitoba and found a small cabin near St. Norbert, a few miles south of the campus and several more from the city of Winnipeg. My cabin was part of a small forest reserve. It was surrounded by enormous ash, linden, and maple trees except where it overlooked the Red River. My cabin had no address, naturally, and I had to pick up my mail at the campus. This residence gave me a wonderful sense of disappearing from everything and everyone I had known in Edmonton. And so for two years I sank more and more deeply into French and into the silence of a forest. I chatted more on campus with botanists and horticulturalists than with English and French professors. Living as I did, so close to civilization, I acquired a sort of weekend woodsiness. Very slowly and very awkwardly Bugnet's story began to emerge in English.

I was lonely most of the time, and sometimes Bugnet's remembered conversations kept me company. From time to time we wrote to each other. He was more than half-blind and was forced to write and read with the help of a large magnifying glass. Following are some excerpts:

April 10, 1972 *This morning I met with an old idea of mine . . . It deals with the origin of the universe. Today many scientists prefer the hypothesis of Georges Lemaitre: a prodigious atom that blew up and is still bursting out. My belief is that before its formation there must have been a preceding entity: motion, which produced Space, and Time, and had such velocity that, at first, it vaporized all the primitive elements. I also believe that today Motion is still the fundamental basis of our Universe.*

February 12, 1973 *I submit to your sagacity a sentence of mine which appeared in* The American Rose Annual *in 1941. "In these times of horribly devastating wars it is a comfort to be able to work with the beneficent creative Power that some call Nature and some call God meaning after all the same thing. The same unfathomable Entity."*

August 21, 1973 *From the depths of my heart and the wuthering*

*heights of my nonagenarian brain I do thank and thank you. Mainly
due to you my last days are filled with public honours.*

*On a different line, my eyes are imitating the Canadian postal
workers and go on rotating strikes. I can't read or write for more than
5 or 6 minutes before they want a rest. They do not hurt, they blurrrr.*

*July 27, 1974 It is not every day that my very old eyes and fingers allow
me to write. You are a very great and good part of me. Before I received
your letter* [about the acceptance of the English translation of *La
Forêt*] *I felt disgusted by the mismanagement of this planet . . . I felt
ready to depart. Your letter changed my mood. Now I want to stay
and go on until I hear of your well earned victory.*

April 21, 1975 [This note was almost illegible.] *My long silence was
due to two stages in the hospital at Westlock. The first on account of
a nasal hemorrage* [sic], *the second to an inflammation in the left foot
where a clot of bad blood had lodged itself. As far as my cataracts, two
doctors, my children and I decided to leave them as they are.*

*You seem to be a glutton for hard work . . . Go to it . . . If you can
come and see me next month I would be delighted.*

My children are taking very good care of my extremely old age.

Immensely grateful to you.

The above note, quoted almost in its entirety, was his last to me.
At this time he was ninety-six. The translation of *La Forêt*, for
which he waited with such resolve, was finished all except for
minor revisions. It would appear about a year and a half after
Bugnet's last note to me when he was ninety-seven.

The translation turned out to be much more difficult than I
had imagined it could be. After each of my chapters was typed
up in English, I had to take it to Paul Savoie (a fine poet and
musician then living in St. Boniface) and to Emily Denney (a
French Professor at the University of Manitoba). They would go
over the materials in French and English and offer variant
wordings of the text. They must have realized I was not a born
translator, but they were patient with me. Frequently I attempted
to do more of an adaptation than a literal translation. Just as

frequently I attempted to include French words for which there seemed to be only the palest of English equivalents. Almost as often my publisher, Maynard Gertler of Harvest House, would remind me that there was always a proper expression in English for a phrase in French. I am now convinced that this is not true, but at the time my knowledge of French was still too rudimentary to appreciate the subtle differences between yes and *oui*.

Here is a passage from Chapter XIII of *La Forêt* that illustrates the problems I was up against. The man speaking is the male protagonist, Roger Bourgouin. Like Bugnet, he is a homesteader and a writer. He is distraught over a sudden bout of sickness in his horse.

> *Bon! Il ne manquait plus que ça. Allez donc écrire un livre avec toutes ces histoires! Maudit cheval! Qu'est-ce qu'il peut avoir? Ce doit être ce maudit froid.*

And here, eventually, is how I translated it.

> *Great! That's the last straw! You try to write a book with all these delightful little things going on. GODDAMNED horse. What the HELL has he got? It's the bloody cold weather, that's what it is!*

Readers will note that I have taken some liberties with the word *maudit*, which means cursed, miserable, wretched. But to a modern audience alert to the fact that Bourgouin is at the end of his tether, such words carry little force. Better entirely to leave in *maudit*–which I insist has no adequate English equivalent. But no, I was not allowed to use French words, so I fiddled with other choices (darned, accursed, blasted?) and decided on goddamned and hell in upper-case letters. To my audience such words would seem mild enough, but to Christians at the turn of the century, or at the time Bugnet was writing his masterpiece, this was not considered to be a mild expression of disapproval; indeed, this was taking the name of Bourgouin's/Bugnet's Lord in vain. However, this curse would be consistent with Bourgouin's moral decline in the forest. Until this scene, he had never used such an utterance in the presence of his wife.

The Forest came out late in 1976. Early in 1977 I received a letter so outraged that it left me speechless. Twelve days later, I received a second such letter. Both were written by daughters of Bugnet. Here is a sample, word for word and letter for letter.

My father for maudit or dam, in La Forêt, Its not even a word, I or any of us has ever heard him use in word of mouth, maudit which in English is dam, was used in La Forêt for one reason only, to show how Roger was loosing some of his Intellectual, Cultural Character which my Father has never lost, in any of his writings or his own Characteristic Standard of Integrity . . . You were not doing this for my Father, (money) I was angry, it has abated, realizing you need prayers to change you and stop you doing any more damage to my Father.

Mrs. Marthe Beauchamp, March 16, 1977

I suppose I should thank my lucky stars that Mrs. Beauchamp's anger had "abated," because if she'd *really* been angry with me I might have suffered a fate worse than Roger Bourgouin's horse. I can only report that her prayers have wrought little change in me.

In my own defence, I should say that the blasphemy on page 91 of *The Forest* is almost the only one in the book—unless you count the word "hell" as a blasphemy. When I had received these denunciations I went immediately to Bugnet to apologize for the trauma I had put him through. He was by then ninety-eight years old, nearly blind, but from all I could see that day, he was completely untraumatized. He did show some uneasiness, however, at the condition of his two daughters, who were showing their disapproval in ways that now I can only imagine.

"It is too bad," he said to me. "They never read very much. They grew up in a place where such things were not encouraged. The books never appealed to them. And now, they are probably looking for you with evil intentions." He laughed and his old eyes disappeared. "I told them that it was not I who uttered these words, but a character of mine."

"Did that help to ease their indignation?"

"No," he said, and we both laughed.

When Georges Bugnet turned one hundred, officials at the University of Alberta decided to grant him an honorary doctorate. His mind was still lucid and he was pleased with the honour. He even prepared a long anecdotal speech for the occasion, which of course he had to do in his head and commit to memory. I heard about the big event from Rudy Wiebe and was surprised that I had not been invited. After all, my articles and translations of his work had in a modest way started the Bugnet ball rolling again. Surely there had been an oversight, perhaps the fact that I was now living in another city. I phoned the organizer. He claimed that I *had* been invited, but that the Sisters had stricken my name from the guest list.

The Sisters. In my mind they had attained the status of Goneril and Regan. With a vanity that only a young scholar could sustain, I felt that I was much closer to Bugnet than either of them. I was determined to attend Bugnet's ceremony. I would drive to St. Albert and get inside even if I had to disguise myself. But of course I wouldn't have to do that because neither of the sisters knew what I looked like. I simply drove to St. Albert, found the hall where the ceremony was to be held, waited until a great many people had entered the church, and approached the front door. An elderly lady stood there receiving guests. For all I knew, she could have been one of the Sisters, but I would not be daunted. I held out my hand and shook hers warmly.

"And you are?" she said with a firm smile.

"Fred Grove," I said. The name, I thought, was appropriate. It was probably the most famous *nomme de plume* in Canadian history. And Bugnet had begun his own fiction writing career with the *nomme de plume* of Henri Doutremont.

The lady greeting me was joined by another, about the same age. "This is Fred Grove," said the first lady.

"I'm from the university," I said.

"Oh," said the second lady, "you must know these gentlemen." She ushered me into the reception hall and there to my horror stood Rudy Wiebe, Mort Ross, and Dick Harrison. My escort said to the four of them, "Do you gentlemen know Mr. Fred Grove?"

"Who?" said Rudy.

"Oh," said the lady with a knowing smile. "Perhaps it is *Doctor* Fred Grove?"

I turned to her just as one of my former supervisors exploded into his glass of punch. "No," I said, "Mister will do fine, thank you." I gave Rudy and Mort and Dick an imploring look and they all smiled back the way blackmailers do at the prospect of a new client.

I looked around for Bugnet. At the upper end of the hall I spied him sitting in a wheelchair surrounded by a quiet group of people. A quiet *watchful* group of people. Two of them were elderly women, though different from the ones who had greeted me at the front door. Were *these* the Sisters? Perhaps. They seemed to regard anyone who came too close to Bugnet with the suspicions of secret service agents.

Oh, Carpenter. How you *do* love to dramatize your own fears. These women were simply well wishers, and what did I have to lose by edging closer to Bugnet so that I could at least whisper my congratulations? I moved closer and closer. I could hear voices in French and English speaking about Bugnet as though he weren't there. I could almost have shouted a greeting. But he was somehow *surrounded* by these people. They were all elderly enough to be his sons and daughters, but how could I be sure? I couldn't just stride up among them, push past them, tell Georges that I was Fred Grove, and expect him to get the message. After all, he was blind and I would just confuse the man.

Someone at a microphone announced that the ceremony would begin. We all took our seats at the front of the hall and the chancellor announced that this was the first time the University of Alberta had ever conferred an honorary doctorate off campus. This was done, of course, to accommodate Bugnet, who was altogether too feeble and arthritic to travel more than a few blocks. After a number of people had delivered their words of praise for Bugnet and his horticultural achievements, his vigorous work for the Lac la Nonne school division, his literary accomplishments, and his courage as an early settler, Bugnet himself was asked to come and add a word or two of his own in English.

I had spent dozens of hours listening to Bugnet's gravelly voice, and so I was used to his rambling, his habit of going back and forth in time as if all of time were present and accessible to him, as if *the order* of things was of little consequence. He could start a story in the twentieth century and finish it in the nineteenth. And this is exactly how Georges approached his address to his audience of perhaps 150 admirers. Feeble though he was, he went on and on and on. We got scraps from his life. The days he had to walk literally all the way around his school district every summer so that he could do his enumerations of eligible students and discuss the problems of the school with the people who sent their children there. We heard about old man Majeau and about his wife who delivered all the children in the area. We heard about his trapline, about his boyhood home in Dijon, about the farmer in Manitoba who tried to make him work for slave wages, about how he had come to know Father Lacombe without ever seeing the man, about the Métis converts who used to pray at the back of the church at Lac Majeau, about how Bugnet acquired seeds for his horticultural experiments from all over the world, about the child he and his wife lost there, about the courage and patience of his *belle épouse* . . .

I looked around me. Something was clearly amiss. I looked at the people closest to me, academics I guessed. They seemed to be confused, whispering to one another. There were others I assumed to be relatives of Bugnet or friends from the nearby French communities, shaking their heads. What the hell was wrong with them? Didn't they know that if they *listened* they would hear the things I had been hearing for more than eight years? But no. The people were plainly confused or embarrassed that this old man was allowed to go on and on about nothing.

Suddenly a tall elderly woman got to her feet and with one parental gesture silenced Bugnet. In the loud voice people sometimes reserve for the hearing impaired, she said, "*You are going on too much!*"

Bugnet's eyes grew wild with alarm. He looked as though he

had been struck. He looked, for the tiniest tick of a second, angry. But anger was useless and he was now, clearly, someone's prisoner. He went silent and the woman who interrupted his ramblings wheeled him away from the microphone.

I bided my time in the old church hall while the luncheon was set up and served. Always Bugnet was surrounded by these vigilant people and I couldn't get near him. But after the lunch was over and some of the well-wishers had said their piece, the sentries became fewer and fewer.

Sentries? Whatever was I thinking about? These were nice Godfearing folk who had greater claims of love for the man in the wheelchair than I. The Sisters were family. I was just a tourist whose encounter with French and francophones was as fleeting as a holiday in Provence. Where was this paranoia coming from? Sentries indeed.

I made my move. I strode up to the small clutch of people standing around Georges, smiled, and eased my way past them to the wheelchair. I knelt down so that my head was only a few inches from Bugnet's. He seemed to sense that someone was there.

I whispered, "Georges, *c'est moi*. Dave."

His mouth fell open. "Carpenter?" he whispered.

"Yes."

"I thought you would not have come here," he said. "They are looking for you."

They are looking for you. Such is the language of intrigue. I knew my situation was perilous, that the same woman who had silenced Bugnet could just as easily have me ejected from the church hall. But something about Bugnet at that moment made me stay. In franglais we had the sort of conversation that some boys engage in beneath a caraganna hedge when the parents are close by. We had some laughs, we made some jokes, we remained in a small way unrepentant.

On my last visit Bugnet said that he wanted to die. He had had a dream. He was back on his trapline near Lac Majeau. He found himself looking into the face of a coyote he had scarcely thought about for seventy-five years.

He told me the following story about the encounter:

You should have seen this animal. He had become trapped in one of my small devices for rodents, and to escape, he had chewed through about half of his own leg. It bothered me to see how much he had suffered and how much he had wanted to live. But when he saw me approach him, I was a young man, and with a young man's resolve to kill any animal that could be of use to me. You know. The pelt and so forth. So I picked up a thick piece of wood to strike him with. He could have snarled and fought against the chain that held him. He could have panicked, but instead he just watched me approach him with my club, and at the last moment, when I moved to the side of him and raised my club to hit him on the head . . . he seemed to squint with his eyes, to squint with his entire head as if anticipating the blow that would put him down. That is how he faced death. He knew it was coming. And he braced himself to face it with what some men could call courage. I dreamt of him last night. We were there again, just like the first time. That is how I want to face death.

Bugnet's problem was that he could not die. He had scarcely had a sick day in 102 years of life. He had made peace with his God. He knew he was declining, his strength was gone, he was completely blind, his legs were no good, and his appetite was waning. He was left with long hours to pray for death and with the hope that he would face it with the courage of his old friend the coyote.

I am being honest when I say I cannot find his death notice. I do know that he died *circa* 1981. Around that time, the rest of the unsold copies of *The Forest* were being remaindered. Maynard Gertler wrote me from his office at Harvest House that if I wanted to, I could buy some of the remaining copies for a pittance. The book had sold about thirty-six hundred copies in four years, then in 1981 or so the market seemed to dry up. I was sure I could sell the rest. So before too long, I received a large shipment of boxes full of *The Forest*. If I'm not mistaken, there were fourteen hundred or so. I moved them into my first house in Saskatoon and kept them in the basement. I sold some through the mail to high schools, and some to universities. I took some to readings and sold them individually. I donated some to the Saskatchewan Writers' Guild and others to university libraries. When I bought my second house, my girlfriend and some others helped me move the remaining seven hundred copies. A few years later my girlfriend and I moved in together to a larger house. Once again she and some others helped me move in the remaining five hundred or so copies of *The Forest*. They cluttered up our store room, and my girlfriend, by now my *belle épouse*, gave me an ultimatum: If I could get rid of these books, she would read the last remaining copy. I couldn't bear to throw them out, so I moved them all into my office. They are there right now, approximately four hundred hardback copies of *The Forest*. My office mate, the Métis writer Maria Campbell, has been very uncomplaining about this state of affairs.

The day came when my *belle épouse* made good on her promise. She read *The Forest*.

"How did you like it?" I said.

"It was good," she replied.

In our back garden we have a Thérèse Bugnet rose. Georges named it after a favourite sister and a grandchild with scholarly inclinations. He developed it himself from the wild rose of Alberta and a domestic variety from Europe. It has the hardiness of the northern wild rose and the delicacy of its European ancestors. It can grow much farther north than any other commercial variety I've encountered. Once Bugnet smiled and said about his rose, "Now I give pleasure to thousands of women."

Lately I've been thinking a lot about this rose.

Reading Bugnet is like reviewing the past two centuries of North American literature in microcosm. When I read his early work, the pieces he wrote just after he arrived in Canada, I am struck by just how much he imposed his European sensibility upon his utterly unEuropean subjects. But when I read his later works, especially his revised version of *Nipsya* (circa 1929) and of course *La Forêt*, I am struck by the many ways he allowed the new world to blow in through his window and work upon his sensibilities. The native grasses and shrubs are there, the original people begin to appear, and of course the settlers. The vast nullity of the winter proclaims itself in all its ranging emptiness. Nature reigns and culture assumes a humbler role in his last two novels. This later work has the feel of the West in it, the vigour and hardihood and mind-numbing simplicity of life in the bush. But the voice is still that of the elegant European listening to the wind and hoping to hear the voice of God. At the end, his thoughts returned to one of his favourite martyrs— not Paul or Peter or even Father Brébeuf, but the trapped coyote who grimaced, waiting for the final blow.

The Prince and the Pelicans

A FEW MILES FROM THE TOWN OF IMPERIAL (that's north of Stalwart), Saskatchewan, about three thousand people are streaming across the grid road into the Last Mountain Lake bird sanctuary: old folks with lawn chairs, school kids with plastic flags, cubs and scouts flashing regimental colours, soldiers in berets, birders with binoculars, tourists with cameras—conservationists all. A flagsnapping wind makes the grass lean one way and the people (from Saskatchewan and therefore stubborn) lean the other. In the centre of a prairie the size of a galaxy, the lake is as long as the Americas. Next to the lake is a sage and gopher field as flat as an ocean (the nearest mountain is six hundred miles west). In the field stands the red and white circus tent on which the crowd is converging. Gulls, hawks, swans, plovers, and cranes drift and teeter overhead. The wind wraps the flags around the poles and sends the ladies' scarves into the far north.

Three oldsters have taken shelter in a straggle of caraganna bushes, huddling like teenagers in a blanket, a man between two ladies. The man says, "I'm just here t'see the copters."

"Oh, you're not," says his wife. "You're here t'see him."

Him. That's how most people here refer to HRH Prince Philip, the Duke of Edinburgh, President of the World Wildlife Fund. He is coming to celebrate the one-hundredth birthday of the Last Mountain Lake sanctuary, the oldest in North America, most recently famous as the nesting ground of white pelicans.

A little background. About ten years ago the white pelican

had declined to sixteen thousand breeding pairs in Canada. In 1978 it was added to the endangered list, and the World Wildlife Fund and Canada Life, whose logo shows a white pelican, mounted a campaign to protect it. This April (1986), when the population appeared to have risen to fifty thousand pairs, it was taken off the list of threatened species. Never before in Canada has this happened.

"This is a once-in-a-lifetime," the lady on the far end of the blanket says. "I collect royalty memorabilia. I have three hundred salt and pepper shakers alone."

From the other side of the galaxy through a tattered sky come three helicopters, scattering gulls and geese. The helicopters rock down and alight. Prince Philip is out at once to a ripple of applause, a tanned handsome man, regal as a ship, wearing an olive jacket, brown slacks, a golden duck pin in his lapel. Flanked by cabinet ministers and honoured guests (two separate categories in Saskatchewan), he strides over to the crowd and chats his way to the platform.

"Look at these," he says to Tom McMillan, federal minister of the environment, indicating a swarm of kids in yellow-and-black tractor caps bearing the logo, "I ♥ No-Name." The Shop-rite in Nokomis has donated them for the occasion. The prince asks the kids what their caps mean and gets seven or eight simultaneous explanations. He asks McMillan, who tries to explain. Is it an Indian name? No, your Highness, uh, y'see, uh . . . and off they go again, past the applauding throng.

The ceremony begins. Gordon Kerr, regional director of the Canadian Wildlife Service, does introductions. McMillan delivers an environmental speech. Robert Bateman, the wildlife artist, presents a painting featuring white pelicans to Prince Philip; in turn, the prince presents a reproduction to Ed Crawford, president of Canada Life. Colin Maxwell, provincial minister for parks, recreation, and culture, reminds the crowd that his home town is Edinburgh. The Duke of Edinburgh smiles.

An eastern kingbird loops the circus tent. All through the ceremony, birds of every description glide by: a marbled godwit, a double-crested cormorant, a ring-billed gull. One by one, one per species, they swoop low across the army of binocular and camera bearers, then swerve back into the wind. A meadowlark, a lesser Canada, a green-winged teal, a Caspian tern.

An attempt to honour these nature lovers with a fly-past? The binoculars and cameras remain trained on the stage.

The prince and the dignitaries have risen to sign an agreement establishing Last Mountain Lake as a national wildlife area. A flotilla of pelicans lifts off from a marsh at the edge of the lake and wheels into the air, drifting in perfect formation around the crowd, riding the air currents in a spiral, the black-edged wings of each bird spread wide for soaring. No one looks up. One by one they bring their wings in and dive, eighteen pelicans, eighteen identical snow-white Chuck Yaegers in perfect control. They pull out at the last moment over the lake and wheel back into the wind. Nothing. The birds have been snubbed.

The prince walks off the stage. He stops to chat with a dandelion field of No-Name caps; he speaks to some legionnaires, who answer back shyly; he waves goodbye. There is, of course, one more thing the birds can do, but they have their orders from Pelican Central. No international incidents today, boys. Bring 'em on home.

The Darker Implications of Comedy

WHEN I WAS A GRAD STUDENT, my test of good comedy was whether it made me laugh out loud in the graduate library. When I read Evelyn Waugh's *Vile Bodies* I broke out into a silly giggle. When I read Rabelais, I broke out into a raucous belly laugh. I suspect my laughter for A *Midsummer Night's Dream* was light and merry. For Mark Twain it was a barbaric yawp. Immediately after reading Alexander Pope, I suspect that I went around with a witty smirk.

But whenever I read Harold Pinter or Samuel Beckett there was this nervous laughter that was anything but joyful. When I finished grad school, I had run the gamut from Shakespearean comedy to restoration and eighteenth century satire to early French ribaldry to frontier humour to black humour and farce. So when I talk about the darker implications of comedy, I'm also trying to get at why my laughter in the presence of contemporary comedy was so uneasy.

Tragedy is easier to define than comedy. Aristotle left us with a full account about what tragedy was, and theorists of tragic literature have used his words as a point of departure to develop more fully their own ideas about its appeal. Theories about classical tragedy often involve a fall from grace of some great and noble figure with a tragic flaw. When we behold our hero's fall we feel pity for his or her suffering and fear for the evil forces that destroyed this noble person. These feelings are excited, purged, and purified in a *katharsis*.

All this came from Aristotle, and much of this theory is still taught in university courses that discuss tragedy. But on the subject of comedy Aristotle either said very little or most of his writing about comedy has been lost. And the field of comic theory is still an open book. (For a good selection of Aristotle's writings on tragedy and a necessarily brief look at his opinions on comedy, see W.J. Bate, ed., *Criticism: The Major Texts* (New York: Harcourt, Brace & World, Inc., 1952), 13-39.)

When I talk about comic writing, I still mean writing that makes people laugh, or at the very least makes them break into a grin. And as I learned in the graduate library, there is quite a range of laughter inspired by comic writing from, say, the comedy of manners as Jane Austen would treat it, to the grotesque and satiric comedy of Mordecai Richler, or the ribaldry of Rabelaisian writers like Robert Kroetsch.

This uneasy laughter of modern-day black comedy is to me the most interesting of all. Reading Guy Vanderhaeghe's *My Present Age* for the first time I laughed my way through nearly every chapter until the last few pages. At the end of the novel I beheld the protagonist Ed alone in his basement apartment, deluded into thinking that his former wife Victoria will be looking for him, unable to go outside and face the world, unable to go to sleep because he is terrified of what he will see when he closes his eyes. He really has reached bottom. He is in the throes of a severe nervous breakdown, and only in the last sixteen lines of the novel does he have a guarded hope of recovery. And his voyage to the bottom has been outrageously funny. I have to ask myself why. In *Modern Times*, Charlie Chaplin gets turned into a twitching, mechanized monster because he has been working at one machine in a factory for too long. Or, in *The Goldrush*, he gets so hungry in his Klondike shack, he has to cook and eat his shoe. I habitually explode with laughter, and again, I am beginning to wonder why.

Here's a short sketch from Harold Pinter. It'll kill you.

Last to Go

A coffee stall. A barman and an old newspaper seller. The barman leans on his counter, the old man stands with tea. Silence.

MAN: You was a bit busier earlier.

BARMAN: Ah.

MAN: Round about ten.

BARMAN: Ten, was it?

MAN: About then.

Pause

BARMAN: Yes, trade was very brisk here about ten.

MAN: Yes, I noticed.

Pause

I sold my last one about then. Yes. About nine forty-five.

BARMAN: Sold your last then, did you?

MAN: Yes, my last *Evening News* it was. Went about twenty to ten.

Pause

BARMAN: *Evening News*, was it?

MAN: Yes.

Pause

Sometimes it's the *Star* is the last to go.

BARMAN: Ah.

MAN: Or the . . . whatsisname.

BARMAN: *Standard*.

MAN: Yes.

Pause

All I had left tonight was the *Evening News*.

Pause

BARMAN: Then that went, did it?

MAN: Yes.

Pause

Like a shot.

BARMAN: You didn't have any left, eh?

MAN: No. Not after I sold that one.

Pause

BARMAN: It was after that you must have come by here, then, was it?

MAN: Yes, I come by here after that, see, after I packed up.

BARMAN: You didn't stop here though, did you?

MAN: When?

BARMAN: I mean, you didn't stop here and have a cup of tea then, did you?

MAN: What, about ten?

BARMAN: Yes.

MAN: No, I went up to Victoria.

BARMAN: No, I thought I didn't see you.

MAN: I had to go up to Victoria.

Pause

BARMAN: Yes, trade was very brisk here about then.

Pause

MAN: I went to see if I could get hold of George.

BARMAN: Who?

MAN: George.

BARMAN: George who?

MAN: George . . . whatsisname.

BARMAN: Oh.

Pause

Did you get hold of him?

MAN: No. No, I couldn't get hold of him. I couldn't locate him.

BARMAN: He's not about much now, is he?

Pause

MAN: When did you last see him then?

BARMAN: Oh. I haven't seen him for years.

MAN: No, nor me.

BARMAN: Used to suffer very bad from arthritis.

MAN: Arthritis?

BARMAN: Yes.

MAN: He never suffered from arthritis.

BARMAN: Suffered very bad.

Pause

MAN: Not when I knew him.

Pause

BARMAN: I think he must have left the area.

Pause

MAN: Yes, it was the *Evening News* was the last to go tonight.

BARMAN: Not always the last though, is it, though?

MAN: No. Oh no. I mean sometimes it's the *News*. Other times it's one of the others. No way of telling beforehand. Until you've got your last one left, of course. Then you can tell which one it's going to be.

BARMAN: Yes.

Pause

MAN: Oh, yes.

Curtain

I think this little play is unforgettable in its tedium. Its plot is as vague as the minds of its two characters. And yet, out of the very aimlessness of the story (if we can call it that), there is something hovering which to my way of reading it comes under the broad category of the darker implications of comedy. Note the ways in which George's alleged departure seem to beg comparison with the last newspaper's departure. Neither man will admit that George is dead, but when that sad conclusion becomes a possibility in the context of their conversation, the newspaper salesman switches back to the business of selling his papers. Apparently George too has been the last to go, so far. Pinter's sketch will suggest this without saying it. Instead, his bleak denizens of the night trade will talk around the topic of death, and if we allow ourselves to ride along with the vague innuendo in the dialogue, we too might begin to think about death.

This woebegone sketch absolutely cracks me up. It invokes a genuine mood of death and desolation and at the same time turns these things into a joke, a parody of human desolation. There's a character in an old W.O. Mitchell *Jake* story, a Mr. Godfrey, who goes about trying to explain prairie humour, particularly the hyperbolic imagination he notices everywhere when he hears oldtimers like Jake talk about the Dirty Thirties. " 'Rust and dust and hail and sawfly and cutworm and drouth are terrible things, but not half as frightening if they are made ridiculous. If a man can laugh at them he's won half the battle'" (100-101). Perhaps this explanation gets us a little closer to Pinter's humour and to the principles underlying modern black humour. But here, a distinction must be made between the kind of frontier humour Mitchell used to excel in during the forties and fifties and what I've called black humour. A Mitchell story of this era, if funny, is usually what I would call White Comedy. Its only engagement with the things appropriate to tragedy (death, for example, or war, or the decline in fortunes of a great wo/man) is through the buoyant extravagance of Jake's imagination or through the innocent eyes of a boy. *Jake and the Kid* is a happy book all about keeping the home fires burning. White Comedy springs from the unexamined exuberance of being glad to be alive. It produces healthy, uncomplicated laughter. And as such, it is almost too salutary for literature.

Too salutary, too much of a surface romp over the perilous voyage through life. During the worst year of my life, the fall and winter of 1969-70, there were only two things I could read: the sports page and W.0. Mitchell. And when my teams began to lose, all I could read was W. O. Mitchell's *The Black Bonspiel of Willie MacCrimmon*. So I owe this writer a real debt of gratitude. It seems to me now that the one thing I couldn't allow when I was in complete despair was *consciousness*. White comedy will give you innocence, prairie virtues, local colour galore, childlike laughter, but nothing to remind us of the world as we know it and sometimes wish it weren't.

Around the late sixties a lot of us in this community (Saskatchewan) began to read the novels of Robert Kroetsch. *The Studhorse Man* comes to mind here. In the midst of a Rabelaisian picaresque, the hero has his brains stomped in by a horse out of control. In the midst of comedy, dark chasms open and close. Using the outward trappings of Rabelaisian wit, satire, picaresque, and the Homeric quest, Kroetsch deconstructs these forms and discovers within them a new sort of comedy with dark implications.

Maurice Charney, in his book *Comedy High and Low*, claims that we inhabit a world so grotesque that "the possibility of tragedy has ceased to exist." This is so, he claims, because we have lost our "belief in a rational order" (107). Here I believe he is drawing on the theories of the dramatist Friedrich Dürrenmatt in his essay "Problems of the Theatre" (1958). Says Dürrenmatt, "Comedy alone is suitable for us. Our world has led to the grotesque as well as to the atom bomb, and so it is a world like that of a Hieronymus Bosch whose apocalyptic paintings are also grotesque. But the grotesque is only a way of expressing in a tangible manner, of making us perceive physically the paradoxical, the form of the unformed, the face of a world without face . . . But the tragic is still possible even if pure tragedy is not. We can achieve the tragic out of comedy. We can bring it forth as a frightening moment, as an abyss that opens suddenly" (107).

Dürrenmatt speaks, infuriatingly, in the first person plural, thereby presuming to speak for an unspecified number of geniuses of his generation. If I can speak for a moment as a writer, and speak only for myself, perhaps I can give my perspective on Dürrenmatt's and Maurice Charney's feeling that tragedy has disappeared as a viable form and been replaced by various grotesque forms of comedy. Tragedy used to treat noble subjects, the fall of the great man or woman from prosperity to ruin. In a relatively democratic age, it is difficult to take seriously the lives of the mighty, unless of course they are dramatized in the soaps or the tabloids, which in themselves are forms of grotesque comedy. It would be very hard indeed to dramatize a tragic soliloquy of Wayne Gretzky pondering the contract that would send him to L.A. or Ronald Reagan pondering when or whether to push the button. There would be some impish impulse within the modern audience that would expect Reagan to push instead the button that flushes his Oval Office toilet. At this moment he smiles and says, "America is strong again." Or worse (and here comes Dürrenmatt again): he pushes the button intended to flush the Oval Office toilet, and instead, the world as we know it is vaporized. Just occasionally over the last few decades we get a distinguished book that we might call a tragedy: Arthur Miller's *Death of a Salesman*, Margaret Laurence's *The Stone Angel*, Malcolm Lowry's *Under the Volcano*. And note, these are not about the fall of the strong and mighty; they are concerned with the fall of the palpably human: a tired old salesman who can no longer be sustained by the lies he has lived; an old tyrant of a woman whose pride prevented her from enjoying the people in her life whom she might have loved; a drunken consul who has plunged almost amorously into the Hell of his own despair.

I find it interesting that all three writers have what I would consider to be a good sense of humour. So does Shakespeare, even when he writes tragedy. It is as if these writers cannot imagine humanity without its double mask of tragedy and comedy. And this double perspective is, for me at least, a pretty good indication of wisdom. I don't trust a writer whose approach to his subject is so earnest or exalted that he can't see the laughable absurdities latent in his material. I distrust him as much as I distrust a writer who plays it only for laughs.

I don't know exactly why Vanderhaeghe's *My Present Age* is still funny the second time through. I don't know exactly why Ed's descent into at least temporary insanity is so funny, or for that matter why I still laugh when I see Charlie Chaplin get brutalized by yet another grotesque emissary of twentieth-century justice. I don't know exactly why Harold Pinter's desolate little sketch is (to me) so funny.

I've only written two or three stories that people might consider to be funny. One of them is a tale about two disabled people who are having a long-distance relationship via tape recorder—a story entitled "The Elevator" (in *God's Bedfellows*). The woman in the relationship is dying and the man is sick of life. I hope that if a young graduate student reads it some day in the graduate library, s/he will laugh. I hope the laughter will be uneasy. I hope s/he will at least briefly think about the brevity of life in a world where death, starvation, and injustice are as close as the News on Channel 12. Sometimes all you can do is laugh.

References

Charney, Maurice. 1978. *Comedy High and Low*. New York: Oxford University Press.

Mitchell, W.O. 1961. "The Liar Hunter." *Jake and the Kid*. Toronto: Macmillan.

Pinter, Harold. 1977. *Plays: Two*. London: Eyre Methuen.

The Morality Tale of Richler's
The Apprenticeship of Duddy Kravitz

PERHAPS YOU ARE FOND OF WILDERNESS LAKES and don't like
to see them commercialized. Or perhaps you are not fond of men
who use the women who love them, or men who take advantage of
helpless people like Virgil, men who climb relentlessly to the heights
of *pusherkedom* leaving a wake of human wreckage behind. Lakes,
lovers, friends in need—they are all in a state of relative innocence
until Duddy acquires and uses them. How, we might wonder, has
a monster like Duddy managed to hold our interest—indeed, our
sympathy—for so many pages?

Mordecai Richler manages this by writing a very moral book;
he demonstrates an intelligent awareness of the moral implications of Duddy's rise to power. Duddy as human being, not
Duddy as mere monster. This is a survival story about a mother-
less boy who sacrifices his dignity to gain status, thereby alienating
the people who nurtured him along the way. As readers, we are
given an opportunity to see into the vanities and absurdities of a
society that encourages, perhaps even guarantees, this destructive
rise to power.

Moses, Richler reminds us, dies before he can behold the
Promised Land; Duddy's soul dies as he attempts to *buy* the
Promised Land. So severely does he alienate his girlfriend, the
gentle and all-giving Yvette, that she feels compelled to seek
revenge upon him. He destroys his relationship with the *zeyda*,
his spiritual mentor and one of the few people he ever came close
to loving. He is at least partially responsible for destroying the

epileptic crusader Virgil, body and soul, a man who served and loved him without hesitation. And the wreckage, of course, does not end here.

The society that encourages Duddy's rise to power is not simply the Jewish ghetto around St. Urbain Street; it is the larger society that contains this ghetto (and Yvette's even lowlier ghetto at St. Agathe). For the time being, let's call it Montreal. We watch as Duddy climbs his way up to discover the hierarchy of this society. At first he thinks the top spot is occupied by Jerry Dingleman, St. Urbain Street's working-class hero. But Duddy looks beyond the racketeer in his apprenticeship to less shady circles and turns to Mr. Cohen, another working-class boy who has become a "somebody," as Duddy would put it. An even more respectable success story would be Duddy's uncle Benjy, a real *mensh*, who is rich, and an intellectual as well. But Duddy rejects Uncle Benjy as easily as he does the Boy Wonder Dingleman.

Working-class Jewish Montreal, like the little army of Fletcher's Cadets commanded by W.E. James, is surrounded and controlled by even more powerful forces outside, not simply their teachers, like the hapless MacPherson, but upper middle-class families like that of Irwin Schubert. At the top is the upper-class financier, Hugh Thomas Calder, who is a bit like the Wizard of Oz in his impotence.

Part of Duddy's apprenticeship is learning this power hierarchy and discovering the rules of the game of becoming a somebody. His first teacher is his father, Max the Hack, who pimps on the side to support his boys. Max is a modern working-class version of the tribal elder who tells the stories to the tribe about where they came from and who their mightiest heroes were, the mythmaker, in other words. And Max's favourite story is the central myth of the ghetto, perhaps any ghetto in North America, the story of becoming a somebody: his riveting account of Jerry Dingleman's rise to greatness by selling streetcar transfers at three cents apiece. Note what happens to his audience of working-class men, Jews and Gentiles alike:

Whenever he told that story Max's face was suffused with such enthusiasm that the men, though they had heard it time and again, sure as they were that it would come out right in the end, unfailingly moved in closer, their fears and hopes riding with the Boy Wonder in Baltimore, who, as Max said, was only a St. Urbain Street boy.

And if Max is the mythmaker, Mr. Cohen, the scrap metal dealer, is the man who spells out the rules of Duddy's game—even more than Uncle Benjy or the racketeer Dingleman. He is a sort of professor of the school of hard knocks.

"We're two of a kind, you know [Cohen says to Duddy]. Listen, listen here. My attitude even to my oldest and dearest customer is this," he said, making a throat-cutting gesture. "If I thought he'd be good for half a cent more a ton I'd squeeze it out of him. A plague on all the *goyim*, that's my motto. The more money I make the better care I take of my own."

It is clear that, by the end of the novel, Duddy has replaced Jerry as the Boy Wonder. Already his father has begun to tell Duddy's story, turning him into another St. Urbain Street myth, a David who leads the fight against the Goliath MacPherson, "an anti-Semite of the anti- Semites, a lush-head." It is equally clear that he has in some sense taken Cohen's advice and become a somebody by being just as ruthless. His apprenticeship has been a process of choosing whose advice to follow in a world that offers a plenitude of advice, everything from his father's words, "Remember, the world is full of shits. Exercise!" to Uncle Benjy's letter, which Duddy reads after his uncle has passed away.

The end of Benjy's letter is very revealing:

There's more to you than mere money-lust, Duddy, but I'm afraid for you. You're two people, that's why. The scheming little bastard I saw so easily and the fine, intelligent boy underneath that your grandfather, bless him, saw. But you're coming of age soon and you'll have to choose. A boy can be two, three, four potential people, but a man is only one. He murders the others.

There's a brute inside you, Duddel—a regular behemoth—and this being such a hard world it would be the easiest thing for you to let it overpower you. Don't, Duddel. Be a gentleman. A *mensh*.

This letter is one of the finest epistles in modern fiction, and a good example of what I referred to earlier as Richler's intelligent awareness of the moral implications of Duddy's rise to power. The letter bespeaks the intelligence and compassion of a character who has "looked back on the man [he] was the year before . . . and . . . was ashamed." Uncle Benjy does not excuse Duddy from moral responsibility. He urges him to choose the role of gentleman, the *mensh*. But in the same paragraph, he also characterizes his society as "such a hard world." In other words, the letter suggests that Duddy is both free to choose and in danger of being determined by a hard world.

In Part II of the novel, Lennie Kravitz, Duddy's pliable older brother, discovers how hard Uncle Benjy's advice is to follow. Lennie tries to become a gentleman by denying his Jewishness and his working-class origins. In the process he ceases to be. Imitating the outward forms of the gentleman, he loses his identity and becomes an easy patsy in the cause of the gentlemen whose friendship he desires so ardently. His betrayers are Irwin Schubert and Andy Simpson. These young men can affect the moral eminence of the gentleman (although Schubert is sometimes even too slimy for that) because they can afford such luxury.

Uncle Benjy had another kind of *mensh* in mind when he wrote Duddy his advice, not simply a man of property, education, and civilized inclinations, but a kind man, a man who is gentle. This latter idea of the gentleman seems truer to the context of the letter, which after all (in spite of Uncle Benjy's denial) is primarily intended as moral advice to Duddy. Historically, the idea of a *mensh*, just like the evolution of the idea of a gentleman, includes not only the social status but also the moral worth implicit in the title. And Richler will scatter enough evidence throughout his fallen world to remind us that *mensh*-hood is not dead. Bernie Altman is a *mensh*; so is Jake Hersh. So, perhaps, are Cuckoo Kaplan and Virgil, at least in their hearts. But they will likely be destroyed by the *pusherkes* they trust.

This perilous world, the one Uncle Benjy tried so hard to rise above, the world that nurtures some boys to become monsters of ambition and destroys the souls of those who trust too much or dream too fervently—I began by calling it Montreal; I will end by calling it the world. Not the earth, the place where a pristine lake lies in the Laurentian mountains, the place where Yvette comes from, or a squalid little patch where the *zeyda* plants his garden, but the world from which we get such terms as worldly wealth and worldly ambition. It seems at first to resemble a Jewish ghetto or a Jewish resort or the office of a *schlock* film-maker. It seems very much like Montreal, *circa* 1957. The world of Duddy Kravitz seems all of these things because Richler, brilliantly, has particularized it so.

But just because he has given to airy nothings a local habitation and a name, and called it Montreal, does not mean that Duddy's world is not our own or that Duddy has cornered the market on pusherkes. Richler's fascination with his St. Urbain Street roots has allowed him to speak with far greater authority—moral authority—about how ambition for worldly gains can corrupt. The truer this novel is to Richler's Jewish working-class background, the more universal its moral illuminations.

Richler reaches the universal *through* the particular, not by an acquired series of mannerisms borrowed from other writers. He engages his theme of human corruption through the particulars of his own boyhood environment. His powerful response to the squalor and comedy of St. Urbain Street and beyond is an act of devotion and love.

Minding Your Manners
in Paradise

W*HEN I WAS A LITTLE BOY,* I had no trouble imagining Paradise in very specific terms. No angels and saints for me. My Paradise would look just like Johnson Lake, a small reservoir fifteen minutes drive from Banff, Alberta, on the Lake Minnewanka Road. It was stocked with rainbow and brook trout that grew prodigiously fast on big nymphs, snails, and freshwater shrimp and spawned spring and fall in the feeder stream. I caught my first trout there and my brother hauled in a six-pound rainbow at the age of six.

When I was in my late teens, I used to fly fish there with my friend Peter Hyndman. We came to Banff to work in the summer partly because of the fly fishing. We were just out of high school and convinced that at the secret heart of the unfolding cosmos was nothing but fun. There were more parties here in one month than we had ever gone to in a year, more unattached girls than we had ever seen. And one or two nights a week, we would declare a health night and go casting on the banks of Johnson Lake. In my first summer in Banff I landed a four-pound brook trout and Hyndman brought in a 5½-pound rainbow. We were becoming legends in our own time, at least among the trout. The girls were another thing entirely.

Each summer we returned and took the well-worn trail around Johnson Lake. Always there was wildlife. One night a very large black bear came down to the lake to drink, or perhaps to stare at the bizarre fly lines whipping through the late summer air. The bear came right up to me. I think I detected an air of disapproval. This was 1960 or 1961, and bears were still so common and innocuous, we hadn't learned to fear them. The bear and I looked at each other from a distance of perhaps twenty feet. It saw that I wasn't going to feed it, and so it lumbered into the jackpine. Hyndman and Carpenter returned to their casting.

A big rainbow was rising just beyond my fly, so I waded in and tried again. Night was falling and Hyndman had brought in his line.

"One more cast," I told him.

This is the most commonly spoken promise by a fisherman, and the least likely to be honoured. I threw out a big bucktail right where the trout had been rolling in the sunset. I let my line sink and began a slow retrieve. My bucktail became an escaping minnow. Jerk jerk jerk, and suddenly the tip of my rod plunged down. A tailwalking olympian had grabbed my fly. He leapt high out of the water, paused for a moment to defy gravity, and plunged back in. He took off for the middle of the lake and my reel whined high and frantic.

"Should I get the net?" Hyndman yelled to me.

"Yes," I must have said to Hyndman, "get the net."

Hyndman got the net and waded over to me while the rainbow cavorted and leapt and took shorter and shorter runs.

"Don't lose him."

Any nonfisher might think that this advice was labouring the obvious. But an angler knows that this is a good luck spell one casts for another.

The rainbow seemed to be tiring. It was pointed down and tailing feebly into the gravel. This passive stance allowed me to ease it closer and closer to the net. Hyndman stretched toward the fish. Dark blue on the back, silver on the sides with a long stripe of pink. It was more than two feet long. It was bigger than Hyndman's 5½-pound rainbow. It was going to be gutted and filled with wild mushroom stuffing and baked for a gathering of at least a dozen friends. It was going to ingratiate me with a half-dozen mountain beauties and be bragged about for years to—

Snap!

A side-to-side motion of its head, the rainbow's way of saying NO to the dreams of a young man intent on becoming a legend. Gone. The king of the rainbows tailed its way back into the deep water as uncatchable as the great white whale.

One of the differences between old anglers and young anglers is in what they tell their friends. We told our friends everything about Johnson Lake. We even took them there. We took our girlfriends there, bating their hooks with big juicy worms and nymphs. Our friends told their friends and their friends told their friends. By the midsixties, this lake, which I felt Hyndman and I had owned, became host to dozens of anglers a day and one or two wild parties each night in the campground. You could hear the voices of folksingers and the sound of guitars and bongos. Always those plaintive undergraduate voices puling about the misfortunes of picking cotton in the hot sun or mining for coal. I was one of those folksingers.

I even remember once throwing a half-finished bottle of wine into the lake. Someone had noticed the approach of an R.C.M.P. patrol car, and I was still under age. I threw the bottle into the lake in panic and stumbled off into the woods. The wine in question was pink, cheap, and bubbly. It was called Crackling Rosé. Does anyone else remember Crackling Rosé?

The problem with Paradise is always the people who go there.

Johnson Lake declined rapidly as a fishing spot, and by the midseventies, it was only good for a few trout of the pan-sized variety. By and by, the parks people stopped stocking it.

By the 1980s I had given up on Johnson Lake. It was overfished, and the only catchable trout at this time seemed to be spawners. An then an incredible thing happened. I was driving by one evening for a nostalgic look at the lake of my youth. At most I'd hoped to get a glimpse of an osprey or a rising trout. I parked my car in a newly constructed parking lot with signs and fancy latrines and picnic benches. I took our old path to the rise overlooking the lake. I looked at the lake.

More accurately, I looked *for* the lake. In the evening light, it appeared to be gone. Perhaps I blinked or shook my head. It *was* gone. The dam at the near end of the lake had burst, leaving behind an ugly grey scar. A prank, I was told later. I raced down to what had been the shore of the lake. I leapt into the muddy cavity. I walked all the way down to the middle of the lake to what would have been one of the deepest holes. All I could find was a trickle from the feeder stream.

How many magnificent memories had that lake held? Standing in the muddy bottom, I had a last look and slowly trudged back. Perhaps a hundred feet from shore my foot dislodged something that made me look down. A wine bottle. It was unbroken and it had no label. But I could tell at a glance from the shape and colour that it had once been a bottle of Crackling Rosé. I suppose it could have been the bottle of some other folksinger, equally drunk and irresponsible, but I think it was mine. I took the bottle, communed with it for a while, and threw it into the garbage container next to my car. But the bottle wouldn't go away. It contained messages from those carefree years. 1960, 1961, 1962, 1963, 1964, 1965 . . . *Michael row the boat ashore, Hallelujah* . . .

This story began with the discovery of my wine bottle. The lake of all memories seemed to disgorge a sad and bounteous flow of them. I had heard often enough that the mind is like a lake that harbours memories in the great Unconscious. But now it seemed to me that the lake was like a huge mind. The more I looked at its vast muddy grey container, the more it poured out the ghosts of its former life, and mine. I was saddened by the usual things. The loss of youth. The loss of that feeling that said the sky was the limit. The inevitable comparisons between the bounteous past and the fishless present. But I think what bothered me most of all was that I had betrayed my lake. I'd made it known to mobs of people unworthy of its great gifts. I'd conspired against my lake by leaving my trash behind and using it merely for my pleasure. I had not taken the time to become my lake's custodian.

Stories like this are legion, and they almost always end in a sad nostalgic sigh. But this one doesn't. A few weeks ago I was in Banff on business. The town had transformed from a place where families came to stay and see the wonders of nature to a place where wealthy foreigners come to shop. Walking down Banff Avenue was an agony. I decided to get out of town and go for a drive. It was more habit than intention that took me out to Johnson Lake, and there I made *another* amazing discovery: it was once again brim full of water and trout! If there's a god that presides over this earthly Paradise, he works for the fisheries department and stocks fish for a living. He is the Johnny Appleseed of the freshwater kingdom. God bless him wherever he goes.

If you should happen to come upon my new old lake, you'll have no problem recognizing me. I'm the balding guy in the belly boat who floats like a frog and hums old folk songs. I'll watch how you dispose of your garbage, if you stick to your limit, whether you bring a ghetto blaster to drown out the sounds of the wilderness, whether you tear up the trail with your ATV. If you fail any of my tests, I will be unforgiving. If you're foolish enough to throw a bottle into the lake, beware. You may not see me *do* anything, but if a huge bear should amble down to your campsite and send you up a tree, don't say I didn't warn you.

Homage to Henry Kreisel

*L*AST NIGHT AT A PARTY, quite spontaneously, Don Kerr, Pat Lane, and I toasted the memory of Henry Kreisel and exchanged some of our favourite Kreisel stories. The mood of the occasion, if not exactly buoyant, was not as solemn as I would have expected. Perhaps our small ceremony felt this way because of the man we were honouring. Some people leave so much behind that even when they die, it feels like they're still around. Henry is one of these people. I can't believe he is entirely gone just as, when I was an undergraduate in his class in the spring of 1964, I could not believe he was entirely mortal.

Professor Kreisel was the first writer of any talent I had ever met. He read the works of Yeats, Joyce, Hopkins, and Eliot so beautifully that their lines burned their way into my memory like holy writ. He was the greatest professor I had ever had.

I was a dismal student, but when I discovered my love of fine books in Henry's class, I fell quite suddenly in love with all of literature. It was very much like a religious conversion for me, and without Henry's knowledge, much less his encouragement, I annointed him my spiritual father.

That summer I had a job as a labourer at the Riverside Golf Course. It was solitary work, raking the sand traps, mowing the greens, setting the hoses on the fairways. Very soon I detected the return of Kreisel's incomparable voice. Lines from Conrad or Hopkins, spoken in Henry's slight Viennese accent, would leap into my head. Lines from his lectures on the figure of the uprooted man in twentieth century fiction. Lectures on the moral responsibility of the writer. Fire sermons on the virtues of tolerant reading. Observations on the influence of photographers' dry plates on modern art and writing.

And then, in the absence of loftier issues, I began to have imaginary conversations with Kreisel on just about anything. Elvis's rendition of "Vive Las Vegas." Or what about this new guy Dylan. Mike Pearson's lousy French accent. The best way to hook a jackfish through the ice.

Kreisel never let me down. All the way from the putting green to the driving range I carried him around in my head like a little walkman. He was wonderful company! I'm sure my boss and my co-workers thought of me as a bit distracted, but of course they never knew why.

One of my failings at that time, I am sure, was never letting him step down from that place on high that I had manufactured for him. I'm less obsessive now. Almost never do I have secret conversations with Henry Kreisel. In my poststudent days I came to prefer conversations with the real man. I came to prefer reading his books, especially his third one, *The Almost Meeting and Other Stories* (1981).

What can we do to fill the void vacated by the death of a great human being? In Henry's case we can read his books. Better still, we can reread his books. And count ourselves lucky if even a trace of that wonderful voice slips back into our thoughts for a brief bit of conversation.

The Word According to Carp:
A Note on Fiction

IMAGINE WE'RE SITTING IN A QUIET BAR. At the next table a woman turns to her friend and says, "Okay, it's my fictive structure. I think he's . . . you know . . . stepping out on me." I think I'd tune her out at this point and spend my time in conversation with you.

Now let's replace "fictive structure" with "boyfriend." Pardon me for being nosy, but I would try to listen to that woman's story. Why is he stepping out on her? How does she know? What advice will her friend offer? What will the first woman do about the wayward boyfriend? You bet your life I'd listen, and perhaps you would too.

Often the stories I like to read are similarly compelling. They remind me of what life is like, what love is like; they explore the moral complexities of being alive right now; they shed light, perhaps even compassionate wisdom, on these complexities without conning us into believing in all the insidious optimism of TV soaps, sitcoms, primetime melodrama, or in the commercially inspired brutality of movies with violent resolutions to human problems. I'm also a bit tired of reading about writers writing about writing unless (like Joyce or Kundera) they do it well. I am tired of self-conscious fiction in which I am invited to behold an author dragging a fictive structure across a page and urged to applaud his wit and learning. I want to read intelligent narratives about believable people and I want to feel something of their lives. And some day soon I would love to write a story so compelling that you turn away from me, and hearken instead to my story as you might hearken to the women wrestling with the sad mysteries of love at the next table.

What We Talk about When We Talk about Carver

GETTIN KINDA DARK OUT," says Robertson.

Honor leans towards me. "Bill says it's—"

"I heard."

"Oi," she says.

"How do we know these guys can shoot?" says Calder. "Maybe they're as rusty as we are."

"They can shoot."

"Hey, Carp, isn't it gettin kinda dark out?" Robertson asks again.

I mumble something and weave through the traffic on 11th Street, eyeing the dark grey horizon, then accelerate for an orange light. Honor clutches the dash. "Watch out," she says.

"It's okay."

In September, in Saskatoon, the evening light seems to vanish like a memory of August. Every fall this happens and every fall I get ambushed by the rapid change. You start thinking about winter for weeks before the Grey Cup or the World Series. It's unsettling. It makes me brood on the brevity of life.

"What if someone hears our shots in the dark?" Robertson asks. He can't quite believe what's going on. "What if they call the cops?"

"There's still some light," I counter.

"Where?" Calder asks.

Honor starts to laugh. The other two join in.

Raymond Carver is coming to Saskatoon. He will arrive tomorrow with his friend Richard Ford. They are bringing their shotguns and expect to hunt with . . . well . . . hunters. I am determined that all of my hunters will make a good showing. They will act like Saskatchewanians. Bob Calder (a biographer) will rediscover that feeling of squinting down the barrel of a twelve gauge, and Bill Robertson (a poet) will cease to wonder how to work his safety catch. He's just bought his first shotgun, an old twelve-gauge double, for twenty dollars. Calder last hunted in 1963. I am the veteran here. I last fired a shotgun four years ago.

"Seriously though," says Calder. "It is pretty dark out."

"Maybe we can use the headlights," I offer. My determination is still strong, but my voice sounds limp.

My determination is strong because in 1982 I stumbled on Carver's stories and felt I just had to meet this guy. Bring him up here for a reading. The question was, how? Our English Department is strapped for visiting speaker funds. Then I read "Distance," one of Carver's stories in *Fires*, and I began to see a way. In this story a young man is about to go goosehunting when his baby breaks out in a crying spell. His young wife suspects the baby is sick, but neither parent knows for sure. She prevails upon her husband to stay home and he misses out on his hunt. The baby stops crying and soon recovers. This story comes to us twenty years later when the marriage is long over.

An idea began to grow. I would invite Carver to read on campus (where I teach on alternate years). Art Sweet, a writer friend of mine, somehow dug up the address of Carver's agent. I wrote to Carver. Let the critics say what they will about "Distance" (. . . a poignant examination of lost bliss . . . a portrait of the raconteur as exile in time and space . . .), its ultimate meaning is a far more fundamental cry from the heart: Will somebody please take me goosehunting?

On January 19, 1986, Raymond Carver answered my letter and said yes, we might be able to work something out.

Honor turns to me. "Do you know the people who own the land?"

"Sort of."

"What are you going to say to them?" she asks.

"I'll just ask them if they mind us firing off a few shells behind their house."

"In the dark," Robertson adds.

"They probably won't even be home."

But the house in question has the lights on. It's a small cozy bungalow built among the aspens and willows. Through the front window I can see the man of the house helping his son with his homework, the woman and daughter kneeling by the fire. The man answers the door.

"Hi," I say, thrusting my hand forward. "I'm Dave Carpenter. I used to camp on that stretch next to you."

He shakes my hand, smiles, and holding his pipe he introduces me to his little foursome. I explain that Honor and I and a couple of friends want to try out our shotguns on a few clay pigeons, shooting into the dunes, of course. The man, who has never seen me until this moment, glances nervously at something in the kitchen. He seems to be gauging the distance between his front porch, where we stand, and his telephone. He strokes his chin, peers at my car.

"Hmm," he says.

But sanity prevails, or something, and my neighbour shows us where to drive out to the dunes in the dark. I take my little Toyota to the top of a small sandhill and point the headlights at a dune about seventy-five feet away. We will release the clay pigeons with a little hand launcher that looks like a long slingshot, aiming these at the small hill in front of us. There is no dwelling in this direction for miles, so the set-up seems safe, if a little unorthodox. I let fly with a few while my friends load up. The clay pigeons are black-and-yellow discs about the size of a small dessert bowl. They glide like accelerated Frisbees into the beams of light and out again. They are visible for about three seconds.

"Gotta be kind of quick," says Robertson dubiously.

He goes first.

"Ready?" I call out.

"Ready."

I send one out a bit high. It skirts the very edge of the headlights' beams.

"Try again."

"Ready?"

"Ready."

I send one across the beam and this time Robertson manages to get his gun to his shoulder.

"Little low?"

"Yeah, try one medium height, straight away."

"Okay, ready?"

"Ready."

This one wobbles in flight, but it's just where Robertson wants it. He fires and misses.

Calder tries. The same thing happens. Robertson tries again. The night reverberates with shotgun blasts followed by "Shit" or "Next time send er higher." Honor tries and nicks one. I try, but no luck. Then Calder, then Robertson. The little yellow saucers pass in and out of the headlights, untouched, safe as UFOs. No one scores a direct hit, but after half an hour of this, we all have a feel for the gun's recoil, and where our safety catches are, and what not to do with a shotgun among friends, so we head back to town. When I've dropped everyone off I discover that my car doorjambs are sticky with dozens of rose hips.

SEPTEMBER 24

Raymond Carver is inspecting a hunting licence in my kitchen. "I am Lee Henchbaw," he says, "and I am from Sass-katchewan."

"No," says Honor, "S's-katchew'n. You don't pronounce the first and last 'a.'"

Carver looks up from the licence. "My name is Lee Henchbaw and I am from Skatchewan."

"S's-katchew'n," says Honor.

"S's-katchew'n," says Carver. "I am Lee Henchbaw and I am from S's-katchew'n." He smiles. "Eh?"

This is the first time I've participated in giving lessons in spoken Canadian: the interrogative "eh" at the end of declarative sentences, the tightlipped "ou" sound that rings Scottish to American ears, the clipped syllables through a puckered mouth, the irresolute shift of the eyeballs as if to ask if life were a federal or a provincial responsibility.

"Have the geese come south?" asks Richard Ford. His south sounds like *sowth* to my ears. There is a trace of Mississippi in his voice.

"South," says Honor, "with the mouth contracted. Pretend you're ashamed of your teeth."

"Sewth," says Ford.

"Sewth," says Carver.

"No, south. Don't open your mouth so wide."

"Mewth so wide," says Ford.

"My name is—" Carver peeks. "My name is Lee Henchbaw and I am from Sass-katchewan."

"Fantastic," says Ford.

"Oi," says Honor.

A lot of geese are down, I tell them. Honor and I have heard them going over for the last three nights, wave after wave.

"Now, Dave, how is this going to happen?" Carver asks. He and Ford are very keen. The thing that makes a spaniel strain at his choke collar is in these guys.

"Pits," says Peter Nash. "A guy named Jake will dig them for us."

Nash is a bearded physician I have known since I was six or seven.

Like Richard Ford, he's in very good shape. At every birthday party, Nash was the kid who had twenty-five per cent more laughs than anyone else. He is still that way. Becoming a father and an ophthalmologist have not visibly altered him. His preparation for this trip meant buying and reading all the books by Carver and Ford he could find in Vancouver. He's as keen as they are. There is an excitement here among us that keeps building. I know that I will scarcely sleep tonight.

"You guys call em?"

"Jake does. He knows what he's doing."

Even though she isn't coming on the hunt, Honor's face is all aglow. She has lived in six states, and it seems to me she has missed the sound of American voices. As most Canadians know, Americans are anything but ashamed of their teeth.

The deal is this: I will take Ford and Carver goosehunting if they will give a joint reading at the University of Saskatchewan for a drastically low fee, what you might call the best kind of free-trade arrangement. I have written to the Saskatchewan Minister of Fish and Wildlife to waive Carver and Ford's alien status so that they can hunt in the Crocus area right after their joint reading, rather than wait around for six days with nothing to do. The reading is slated for September 25, but around Crocus, Saskatchewan, Americans aren't allowed to hunt until October 1. Duke Pike, the minister in question, is a circumspect man who believes the universities and intellectuals are out to get him, or so people have told me. Predictably, our request is denied. He suggests we reschedule the whole damn event, which at this point is impossible.

I had to get two extra hunting licenses. Enter Art Sweet and Lee Henchbaw, both writers. They haven't hunted a day in their lives, but for the cause of literature, they put their asses on the line. Art Sweet, among other things, is a very fine one-handed guitarist. Emergencies seem to be his stock in trade. Lee Henchbaw is a possessed poet; he seems perpetually astonished by life. He handed me his hunting licence and announced his intention to write a Raymond Carver poem. Perhaps Carver will write a Lee Henchbaw poem. Lee is beset by verbal overload. He may burst before he jumps on his motorcycle.

"I am Lee Henchbaw, and I am from Sass-katchewan," says Carver, all night long, through a bout of insomnia.

That's the part I remember from Wednesday night. What Honor remembers is quite different. None of this talk about goosehunting. She remembers Nash at the stove frying a large batch of fresh-caught smelts in egg and bread-crumb batter. She remembers a series of confessions during our meal. Ford was first: "You know the last words my mother ever said to me? She was on her deathbed. She said, 'Richard, will you please stop asking me all those questions?'" This remark inspired other confessions about pain, death, and worry. Carver talked about how terrified he was when Tess Gallagher (his partner) had to have an operation for cancer. Nash told us about his fears upon discovering an advanced melanoma on his right arm. I'm sure I put in my two cents worth. In my youth I was very enthusiastic about pain.

Just before we fell asleep, Honor marvelled about the evening's talk. "Here's four guys, none of them trying to sound liberated, talking about their *feelings*." She was still all aglow. "I've gotta tell Lorna."

SEPTEMBER 25

From B.C. to western Saskatchewan there is a hurricane warning, rare for these parts. In Lethbridge it has rained four inches; in Calgary it has snowed twelve. In Saskatoon the wind buckles the elm trees near the campus and dismantles election campaign signs. For the first time in Saskatchewan history, there are New Democratic Party signs on the lawns of the wealthy. The rain has turned to sleet, but not yet snow. Carver and Ford are having lunch down the street from my house, Nash and I making sandwiches for the road, when the phone rings.

It's Honor at her studio. Jake's been trying to get hold of me. He thinks we should cancel the trip. I tell Nash. He can see I'm very worried; I've got that why-me look.

"Let's not phone Jake," he suggests. "Let's pretend we never got the message. Let's just go."

"Yeah." Desperate dilemmas require desperate solutions.

We stare at each other. The reading is two hours away. Perhaps more than a hundred students, writers, profs, and book lovers will be getting ready to brave the storm for this event. I am holding my head in my hands, moaning something about the unfairness of life. In Saskatchewan that often means weather. I rail for a while, and Nash, undaunted, counters with his own philosophy: that life is random, not fair or unfair. "The test is always how well we deal with the randomness!" he cries. He's in an impassioned state of inspiration, like the wind outside. We seem to be caught in the plot of a Russian novel here.

We decide to phone Jake. Jake says exactly what I had feared: "Yiz guys better call the whole thing off, eh. I mean my brother an I we can't even get a four-wheel drive into the field, dig the pits. You can't get no vehicle nowheres near there."

"Jake, I can't call this whole thing off. These guys have come a long way."

"Well, I dunno what I can do. We got two inches a rain down here in the past twenty-four hours. Fields an roads solid gumbo."

"Are the geese down?"

"Yeah."

"Could you show us where they're flying?"

"Yeah, but yiz'll all have t'walk some."

"What's the forecast?"

"Pissin."

I look at Nash, who holds a knife heaped with mayonnaise in one hand, a slice of bread in the other. He does not seem rattled. "Well, Jake, we're coming."

This is one of those days when you simply worry your way from one decision to another. I will worry about the reading till it's happening, worry about not telling Carver and Ford that Jake wanted to cancel, worry about the condition of the highway, worry about the sufficiency of everyone's rain gear, hit the sack and worry about how to get to sleep. I will worry about setting back Canada/U.S. literary relations by twenty years and giving Saskatchewan a bad name. In my dreams my parents will tell me that they told me so, and I will worry about where they went wrong with me. I am leading five guys to their deaths. I will really worry about that one. Outside, the wind howls, the rain lashes, and life's randomness proclaims itself all day long.

The classroom is full, hushed. People's foreheads, hair, and coats are streaked with rain. The linoleum is splattered with mud and yellow elm leaves. We can hear the wind outside, and this sound precipitates, it seems to me, a cozy smug feeling. The best writers and some of the best artists in the province are here. A contingent of twelve people has driven all the way from Regina against this wind and into the sleet. The classroom seems to bristle and glow. People are still gasping from that last dash across the quad. Guy Vanderhaeghe *(My Present Age)* is chewing a huge pink wad of bubblegum. Barbara Sapergia *(Foreigners)* huddles into her coat and breaks out in little shudders. Pat Krause *(Freshie)* and Byrna Barclay *(The Last Echo)* babble about how cars were swaying in the wind fifty miles south of Saskatoon. Anne Szumigalski *(Dogstones)* spreads her wool shawl out around her like a tea cozy and smiles her four-year-old girl's smile. Patrick Lane *(Linen Crow, Caftan Magpie)* looks straight ahead as several women talk to him. "You better believe it," he says. "You better believe it." Geoffrey Ursell *(Perdue)* strokes his beard, folds his arms, surrounds himself with reflective silence. Lois Simmie *(Pictures)* looks at Carver with undisguised adoration. Elizabeth Brewster *(Selected Poems, 1944–1984)* hurries in at the last moment, huddles into the last available chair. Lorna Crozier *(The Garden Going On Without Us)* is the last one in the room to stop laughing. Art Sweet (fiction writer, guitarist, poet) and Bob Calder *(Rider Pride)* look as though they are seconds away from opening kickoff. And (words bouncing off his brain like ping-pong balls) Lee Henchbaw is perhaps thinking, I am Raymond Carver and I am from Port Angeles. Nash's head goes around and around 360 degrees so he can see everything. This is show biz and he knows it. Bill Robertson *(Standing on Our Own Two Feet)* gawks impatiently, as though he wants to get in a dozen windsprints before the reading begins.

"Ladies and Gentlemen," I begin. My voice seems to be talking and I'm helpless to do anything with it. "I suppose I was hired on here because I am a regionalist. That means I'm interested in the writing that has been done around here. Well, angling for Raymond Carver and Richard Ford has been a very good exercise for me, because I'm now willing to admit that, yes, some very good writing is going on outside of Saskatchewan."

Polite laughter.

Get on with it, Carpenter.

Carpenter *(Jokes for the Apocalypse)* gets on with it. A warm applause, at long last, for Richard Ford. He is lean, pale; his face flickers with sensitivity. (Elizabeth Brewster confides later to me that he certainly is "cute.") His voice has gathered intonations from all his wanderings, from the Deep South, to the industrial Northeast, to the Midwest, and to the Old West, where he now lives.

> I was standing in the kitchen while Arlene was in the living room saying goodbye to her ex-husband, Danny. I had already been out to the store for groceries and come back and made coffee, and was standing drinking it and staring out the window while the two of them said whatever they had to say. It was a quarter to six in the morning.
>
> This was not going to be a good day in Danny's life, that was clear, because he was headed to jail.

Thus begins "Sweethearts," Richard Ford's latest story in *Esquire* (August 1986). For half an hour, the audience wraps itself up in Richard's story and wears his voice like a comforter as the wind buffets the window panes. It occurs to me that being read to is a great luxury, especially on a stormy day. The audience responds warmly, and I wonder if the public Carver can be half as captivating. On the page, of course, he is, but this is show biz.

Raymond Carver stands six feet two, a big-bodied man apparently comfortable with his size. He has a way of going quiet and quizzical and at such times reminds me of that awkward brainy kid in grade six. Or as an undergraduate, he would be the shy, dishevelled guy in the corner, lost in thought. A bit like Lee Henchbaw. They both have an abundance of curly hair, which I envy, and it seems to announce something luxuriant in their minds that cannot stop growing. They are working-class men right down to their cigarettes. Both recall hard times and domestic strife all the way back to childhood. But the man at the lectern has now become Raymond Carver, and Lee is perhaps fifteen years away from becoming Lee Henchbaw. His first poems have just appeared, but he is still young enough to ride a motorcycle. In a few years, he will be up there at the lectern, launching one of his books. In a few more, if he remains devout and disciplined, he will become a small part of literary history. Then fade with the rest of us. Clay pigeons flashing through the headlights of the cosmos. The critics take their pot-shots in the dark, and usually miss, and then we all die. I wonder if Nash would agree with this. The weather breeds such ruminations.

Carver is absolutely unhistrionic, soft spoken, humble by disposition rather than design. He begins by asking the people at the back of the room if they can hear. But perhaps they can't hear him yet, so they just stare back at him. He asks again. They stare back again. Carver is in Saskatchewan, where seldom is heard an extrovert's word. People in readings don't raise their voices if they are in the audience. That would be showing off. So Carver begins, plainly worried. He reads from one of his recent *New Yorker* stories ("Whoever Was Using This Bed," April 28, 1986). In about one minute, with the line, "What in God's name do they want, Jack? I can't take any more!" he has us. Soon, more than a hundred sodden people are howling with laughter. The characters grope through the night for words to put on their fears and their despair, but throughout the story there is this laughter. I can't help wondering, is this the man Madison Bell attacked (in *Harper's*, April, 1986) for being a "dangerous" influence on American short story writing? Another studiedly deterministic nihilist? Bell argues that the reader is drawn into a Carver story "not by identification but by a sort of enlightened, superior sympathy." The audience here goes from rib-aching hysteria to rapt attention as the narrator and his wife talk in bed at five or six in the morning about whether one would unplug the other from a life-support system if s/he were suffering unduly. Is this conversation the sort of thing the genteel Mr. Bell would call nihilistic? Am I missing something? When I read *Cathedral* (upon which Bell focuses his attack), did I miss out on all that impoverishment of the human soul? Maybe like Bell I should have been saying to Carver's characters, "I understand the nature of your difficulty; how is it you don't?"

I decide, at the moment of applause, that the genteel Mr. Bell suffers acutely from a superiority complex and that he wouldn't know a compassionate story if it goosed him in the subway. This, of course, isn't exactly a meditated judgement, only a reflex. But I can't escape the conviction that Carver is telling our story, however squalid or despairing, and we find ourselves having slept in his narrator's bed. The applause continues for a long, long time. You'd think Tommy Douglas had come back from the grave.

The crowd ascends to the tenth-floor coffee lounge and descends upon the Americans. They have to clutch their styrofoam cups close to their chins, and guard them with the other hand. Saskatchewan has come to pay court to them. The mood is suddenly effusive.

In fact, for this place at least, it is wildly effusive. I feel like one of those Broadway producers who chews on cigars and shouts at the last minute replacement for the leading lady, "Go out there, Mabel, and break their hearts!" My God, I keep thinking, I've got a hit on my hands.

An hour later it occurs to me that I have a hit and no pits. No pits, no geese. No geese, no reciprocity from us to them. Carver and Ford have waived a considerable sum in fees and expenses to come here and shoot. Which makes me (in collusion with the weather) one of the all-time welchers in Canadian literary history.

"Say, ah, David," says Carver in the front seat, "that's a heavy rain coming down. Is that normal for here?"

"Well, no, Ray. Actually it's a real heavy one."

He looks out at the countryside flashing by in the fading light. Ford is silent. Perhaps he is looking for geese. So far we have seen none.

A minute later, Carver says, "Say, ah, David, that's a heck of a wind out there. Is that normal?"

"Well, no, Ray. Actually it's quite unusual for up here." I've said nothing about the absence of goose pits or Jake's phone call. I've said nothing about the hurricane warning. The one blessing is that this pummelling wind is behind us.

"About these pits," says Ford. "Aren't they likely to be a bit on the wet side?"

I tell a censored version of the grim facts. There may be no pits at all. There can't be any digging in the farmers' fields until they've managed to take in their crops. And in this weather, digging is impossible, walking "a bit dicey." I suppose my nervousness has begun to show through.

"David," says Carver, "I'm excited. Richard here is excited. I feel I'm on some sort of adventure. If I even see some geese tomorrow and get a bit of walking in, that'll be fine. I'll have had my fun. So don't worry. Hell, we're all on an adventure here."

I nod, very much relieved, and repeat Nash's words on contending with the randomness of life. This view, the kind of advice an ophthalmologist may have to give to a patient on occasion, rides well with us all the way through the storm and down to Crocus. Nash is no doubt spreading his gospel of adventure in Calder's vehicle. The six of us have become soldiers of fortune. We face the howling infinite together. This last statement probably sounds self-dramatizing. Such is the language of epic.

Saskatchewan and Carver. Why the instant love-in? He's a fine writer, but many other fine writers (Margaret Atwood) and scholars (Northrop Frye) have bombed in Saskatoon. First we single out Carver's books for praise, then, in about two minutes of reading, we respond just as warmly to the man. Better readers (W.O. Mitchell, Erin Mouré, Graeme Gibson, Michael Ondaatje) have worked harder to warm up an audience. And wasn't Ford's story a bit tighter? It seemed so during the reading. Should we not, then, be more circumspect about Carver's books, such as Mr. Bell has advised? Some of us are no doubt aware of Carver's excesses even as he reads, but no one voices any critical disapproval later on, after the event. Is the Carver/Ford reading one of those obsequious moments, then, in which a bunch of Canadians grovel at the feet of someone who has made it big in America? I can't absolutely deny there was at least a trace of this feeling in the room. But

I don't think the excitement at the reading was impelled by mere obsequiousness. I think much of the laughter, for instance, was that of recognition, that the agonies of Carver's two insomniacs, their dread of a prolonged death, were to a great extent our own.

Mr. Bell seems distressed over the language of many Carver stories, concerned as they are with "the predicaments of bluecollar workers verging on the skids." What rankles at Bell's sense of literary propriety "is a slightly artificial lowering of diction" to "describe a very sophisticated pattern of events."

I find this argument irksome.

I read Carver's stories for many things: among them that strange dependency of squalor and humour in the tone, the equally strange dependency between the ordinary and the numinous, and that way his characters have of telling us far more than they mean to. Who says this is an *artificial* lowering of diction? Is it artificial because plain-speaking people are not generally competent to talk about the complexities of their lives, or at least report their own stories in a suggestive way?

Carver brings to Saskatchewan the suggestive richness of plain speech. Saskatchewan greets Carver with a tradition of plain-speaking. Our greatest works of fiction (Sinclair Ross's *As For Me and My House*, W.O. Mitchell's *Who Has Seen the Wind*, Wallace Stegner's *Wolf Willow*, Guy Vanderhaeghe's *Man Descending*, for example) are unapologetically realistic. Perhaps this adherence to the imperatives of realism doesn't seem surprising to readers unfamiliar with the Canadian West. But if we look at the finest Alberta fiction over the same fifty years (Howard O'Hagan's *Tay John*, some of Rudy Wiebe's Indian stories, most of W.O. Mitchell's Alberta fiction, and Robert Kroetsch's *Badlands*, for instance), we get myth, epic, tall tales and other kinds of comedy in the hyperbolic tradition, romance, postmodern satire—anything but realism.

When Albertans were forging the Social Credit Party out of the remains of the United Farmers Movement and the biblical prophesies of William Aberhart, Saskatchewanians were creating the C.C.F. Party. Compare the mythopoeic style of Aberhart's or Manning's speeches (in church or in the legislature) with the hardnosed realism of Tommy Douglas's speeches, and you have a rough idea of what I'm talking about in the literature of these neighbouring provinces.

Nowhere I know of are the niceties of middle-class diction, the borrowed jargon of deconstructionism, the linguistic excesses of romantic fiction less relevant than in Saskatchewan literature. And in Carver's stories, I suspect. There is a correlation here, and it shows up in the language: the rhetoric of hard lessons, limited expectations, toughminded compassion. We have known hard times and from this knowledge comes our regional pride. Western Albertans are mountain snobs, Vancouverites like to feel sorry for the rest of Canada, Victorians are flower garden snobs, Calgarians (to use some of W.O. Mitchell's distinctions) are horsey snobs, Edmontonians are sports and progress snobs. Saskatchewanians are for the most part endurance snobs. They are sure they can endure more drudgery, worse winters, more absurdities from Ottawa, worse droughts, a greater sense of nullity from looking at flat surfaces, more defeats to their football team, than anyone else in Canada.

Saskatchewan literature, as Robert Kroetsch has said (perhaps lamented is a better word), is inward looking. The experiments of Marquez, Borges, or Barth or Calvino, which were emulated and imitated by so many writers in other parts of Western Canada, came to nothing in Saskatchewan. At their best, Saskatchewan writers like Lorna Crozier, Andy Suknaski, Guy Vanderhaeghe, or Ken Mitchell preserve a strong connection to their regional origins. So have Sinclair Ross, John Newlove, and a number of eminent former residents. The language of postmodernism seems to be of passing academic interest, having so little to do with Saskatchewan idioms, in our mouths an artificial language. The complexities of our lives are rendered in a native language; the complexities of our collective imagination are rendered in terms that emerge from our own dreams of our place. We are stolidly unimpressed with whatever happens to language when it gets deflected and convoluted by life in the big city. There are some important exceptions to this overall picture (the poetry of Ed Dyck and Anne Szumigalski, the fiction of

Geoff Ursell), but even these three mavericks have written extensively and successfully out of their Saskatchewan experience. There is still a grainy, marshy smell to some of their most adventurous work.

For the most part, we are plainspeaking, and this explains to me the recent popularity of Carver's visit. He managed to affirm something about our own idiom by speaking so well in his.

Robertson goes from room to room in his underwear. Rallying the troops. "Five-thirty tamorra mornin," he growls. He sits on anyone's bed, at home wherever he goes. "Hell," he says after a pause, "it'll be just like summer camp, first night. We'll all stay awake an talk about sex."

The wind shakes the motel basement windows as we sit around; the rain seeps in and sprays anyone beneath the screens. We lay out our rain gear, our long range magnum shells. The geese will be flying high, spotting us easily. Carver and Ford, both insomniacs, will room together, Calder with Robertson, and I with Nash. Carver wants to be roused by five. He has a little coffee maker and wants to get it going so we can all have a shot. Nash warns me of his snoring, claims he can shake a building with it. He tosses me some earplugs.

Maybe Robertson is right. It is a bit like summer camp. Nash sleeps like a baby, but I review the day, try to think about lying in mud, revel in the success of Ford and Carver's reading, blink and ruminate all night long. Perhaps I doze for half an hour, but when the alarm goes off at five, I'm as galvanic as an electric owl.

SEPTEMBER 26

Five o'clock in the morning. Ford mumbles, "Why the fuck do we have to get up so early?" He sounds very much like a boy in Mississippi embarking on his first hunt. He will demonstrate later that he is anything but a greenhorn.

Ray makes pot after pot of strong filter coffee. Each pot is a cup. Each cup gets passed from room to room, from bed to bed. The empty cups come back to Ray and he has another to send down the line. Breakfast is doughnuts, several kinds. This is our gift to Ray, because apparently he is addicted to them in the morning. Our rooms are littered with crumbs and spattered with coffee. We drag on our clothes, layer after layer. I start with long johns, then thick pants and T-shirt, then K-ways top and bottom, then thick wool sweater, then canvas hunting coat and hat. Most of what I wear is what I've worn for decades on these trips. My pants are torn, my coat stained and stiff with goose and duck blood. Calder looks about the same to me, and Nash and Robertson. We reek of barley and odd prairie smells. An old fellowship seems to reemerge with the donning of this brown canvas coat.

Carver and Ford have newer waterproof clothes, and Ford actually looks dapper in his. We'll have to do something about that, I think, but I can't imagine what. Guns in hand, we lurch and waddle through the rain and mud to Jake's house. He meets us with a friend in his garage. It is brilliantly lit inside. He too has doughnuts and coffee, knowing of Carver's addiction.

"She's colder'n a sonofabitch out there," says Jake. "Sock 'er down, eh? It's a long time till dinner."

The garage is huge, full of duck-hunting equipment and all-terrain vehicles. The lighting is so intense that we stand around in embarrassed silence, yawning, savouring the last dry surfaces we will feel for many hours.

Four of us go in Jake's jeep, three follow in Calder's truck. We take the highway about ten miles south past the town of Horizon, and Jake pulls over and parks on the shoulder. "Far as she goes," he says, knowing full well that nothing with wheels could get a hundred yards on the side roads.

The sun makes faint grey streaks on the eastern horizon, but it's still dark where we sit in the jeep. Suddenly we stumble out onto the road, Jake in the lead, swearing. "Timed er wrong," he says. "Shit. "

I hear choruses of falsetto barking, and then I see them: wave after wave of geese lifting off the slough and pouring over the road, low but out of range. The sky is exploding with them: greater Canadas, lesser Canadas, specklebellies, snows, and many ducks.

We lurch down the road in single file. We are almost at the edge of the flight path, but it's getting lighter and there is no place to hide. The mud builds up around our boots until each foot wears ten pounds of Saskatchewan gumbo. Our breath comes hard. The wind and rain lash into our faces. My glasses need windshield wipers.

Jake and Ford and I manage to reach a point on the road about half a mile down from the vehicles. Jake and Richard begin to blaze away, standing on the road. I have only a sixteen gauge, so I keep on trudging into the middle of the flight path, Nash right behind me. I hear guns going off but I keep on going till I reach a culvert I can hide behind. Nash and Ford fire down the road and double on their first goose. A lone duck tries his luck swinging low over the culvert, and I bag him. He falls on the road with a squelch and he's dead before I stuff him into my coat pouch. This is how you always want it to happen, a clean kill.

Calder and Robertson are nowhere in sight. Jake has headed back into town. Carver and Ford lie in the ditch back down the road two hundred yards from me. Nash trudges slowly out into the north field and disappears over the edge of the world. It is every man for himself, and the birds are wise to our plan, such as it is. They spot us a mile off and fly high over our heads. We blast away and they keep on flying. This is called pass shooting. The geese pass, the hunters fail.

By nine o'clock we still have only a duck and a goose, apparently dispatched by Calder as it tried to escape. This I learned later; Calder and Robertson are still missing in action.

The wind has been playing with us as we lie in the mud. By ten o'clock it rises up like a wendigo and blasts sleet and rain into our faces. To remain as innocuous as possible, Ford and Carver lie face down in the mud, and when the geese fly over, they leap up and try to fire as their feet slide beneath them. I shoot occasionally, but it's clay pigeons in the dark again, so I huddle down by the culvert to try and keep my back to the wind, checking every minute or so for new flights of geese. Nash reappears over the northern horizon like a perambulating scarecrow, then disappears. He moves to keep warm.

At last the wind and sleet are unbearable, so I head for a clutter of grain bins out in the field. Crouching behind these bins is a bit better, but I'm still so cold my teeth chatter. One of the bins is actually an old wooden granary. I peek inside. It is empty, which surprises me. But because of this weather, half the farmers haven't been able to harvest their grain, thus the empty bins. I turn the lock and go inside, and at last, with the wind shrieking all around the bins, I begin to warm up. From time to time I can hear geese flying over the bins but my gun leans against the wall. This soldier has bid goodbye to the wars.

Then I smell something, an offering from below, sour and rotten. *Skunk.* I'm out of there in about four seconds and back to my culvert.

By eleven Nash returns, three large geese and a duck hanging over his shoulder. He is tired, happy, and very wet. We push on down the road. Carver and Ford get up out of the mud, and I see now what they are made of. From lying face down in the mud, Richard has acquired a carapace of bluish clay over his face. His clothes are filthy. Carver is just as muddy and he is bleeding rather badly from two cuts in his left hand. We look each other over for a while. We are the remnants of a defeated army, trench warfare, *circa 1917* when the Americans entered the fray.

And the Americans haven't yet admitted defeat. First Carver, then Ford, then I, begin to build a large duck blind out of chaff. I gather the chaff, hand it to Richard, who gives it to Carver. Back and forth we go, the geese flying cautiously high. By noon we have what resembles a huge bird's nest, big enough for three hunters. Ford and I are puffing, Carver close to exhaustion.

It's time for lunch. We shoulder our guns and slowly trudge the long mile to the vehicles. Robertson and Calder greet us by the truck. They've had no luck at all and seem discouraged, especially Calder. When he had to dispatch the wounded goose by wringing its neck, he discovered something about himself. Over the twenty-three years between this hunt and his last one, he had acquired a conscience about killing things. We discussed this later. We all shared a real affection for those geese we hunted—apart from their value as food or quarry. This affection is what Faulkner refers to as loving the creatures you kill. But Calder's conscience took him one step further. The killing felt unbearable to him and he had lost the hunter's instinct.

On our last fishing trip, Calder had always been the driving force, the keener, the strongest courier over the last portage. I had been the one to lose sleep worrying about bears and the first to tire after a portage.

"Can't cut er," says Calder, plainly discouraged.

"But Calder, you've been an administrator. You've been in the dean's office for God's sake. You're not supposed to have a conscience any more."

He gives me a sardonic grin. There is nothing more to be done. Like prehistoric creatures who dimly feel the end of their epoc, we slither into Calder's camper and head home for lunch. Some of them curse Jake, though it's not his fault. We curse the weather and dream of showers and more hot coffee.

While the others shower, I head over to Jake's garage and find him in the grease pit. Four other guys stand around talking with Jake as he works. I'm carrying the four geese and two ducks. "Where can I get them cleaned?"

"Goose plucker's daughter," says an old fellow. "Over at Horizon."

"Does she work fast?" I ask.

Jake sticks his head out of the grease pit and smiles. "Oh, she's fast all right."

The men chuckle.

"You go t' Horizon, Dave. Doris'll take care of ya."

Again, tribal chuckling from deep in the belly.

"No crap, Dave, you're gonna meet a real pretty girl, eh?"

By the time I get back to the motel, some of the guys are eating, some showering. When it's my turn, I simply hold my K-ways and canvas coat under the shower until the clay peels off and down the drain. The bottom of the shower is plugged with three inches of mud. Changing into dry clothes is a pleasure worthy of a voluptuary.

Finally, after lunch, as the others rest, I load up the birds and take along Robertson for protection. This Doris woman sounds threatening to me. I've turned her into a monster of Gothic proportions in my own mind, and Bill is very curious. He assumes she is merely old and disfigured.

Horizon is a ghost town. Two families remain. It used to have hundreds, but bad crops and large farm corporations seem to have driven out the residents. Doris's place is a one-storey frame shack next to a demolished house and barn on the edge of town. Her backyard is the endless prairie.

I think of Mrs. Bentley from *As For Me and My House*, how each day she would listen to the wind and dust sift through her house. At one point she calls the wind "liplessly mournful." I don't understand this phrase, but it haunts me.

I knock on the door.

Doris answers. She is about five foot two, ash blond, twenty-five, her make-up a bit on the heavy side, barefoot, and gorgeous. "Hi," she says with a bright smile.

At three o'clock, fed and rested, we cram into Calder's camper and try our luck one more time. We park the truck by the road again, and off go Nash, Ford, and Robertson. Nash will stick to his perambulating; Ford and Robertson will crouch in the duck blind.

Carver tries the muddy road again, but it's no go. He has a torn muscle or a charlie-horse in his left groin, a bum right leg, a swollen left toe, and from compensating all day long, a bleeding blister on his right foot. We've helped him bandage up his hand and his foot, but the man is on his last legs, sweating and hobbling in the mud. "You know, Dave, I think if I try this road again I'm just not gonna make it. I think maybe I'll stick by the highway."

We stop and look around. The other three have gone on ahead and disappeared. The rain has almost stopped but the wind persists. "I think I'll stick by the highway," he says again. "I think I'll try my luck here." A while later he says, "I tell you, Dave, I could sure use a Coca Cola. Where do you think we could get one?"

I have the keys to Calder's truck. There is Horizon and Bean

Coulee just a few miles down the road, and of course Crocus in the other direction. We head for the truck.

"If I could have a Coca Cola," says Carver, smiling painfully, "I think I could maybe make it through the afternoon." Perhaps this is how Carver talked about booze in the bad old days before he took the pledge. I too am thirsty. Before us looms a huge frosty bottle of Coke. The prairie has become a desert, and that ultimate American symbol, the Coke machine, our oasis. By five o'clock or so, we are beat but we simply will not acknowledge this. Like I say, Horizon is a ghost town. We discover it has no store. Bean Coulee hasn't even a Coke machine. We head back toward the muddy road, thirsty as hell. But before we reach it, Carver spots a huge wedge of geese flapping over a gravel road. A *gravel* road. This means it can be driven on. We try it out. The truck moves slowly down the road; wet though it is, the tires grip. We drive beneath another large flock of honkers. Carver clambers out and checks the ditch. It's almost too dark to shoot, but we have tomorrow morning. Carver and I discover ample patches of weeds and standing grass, deep patches where we can hide in the morning. There is a light in Carver's eyes, a youthful look. "Goddam, David, this is it. We can come here tomorrow morning. Five o'clock. This is the place. Would you like to join me here tomorrow morning?"

"You bet," I say. "If they're flying low, I'm with you." My gun is built for close-range stuff, so we seem destined to try our hand at this new road. To the north are several huge fields of swath. To the south across the road is a large slough, and string after string of geese pouring into it from the fields. The whole dark sky is honking.

"You bet," says Ray. "This is it. This is the place. You know what? I'm comin' here tomorrow morning. Would you like to come?"

We arrive at dark on the mud road to pick up Nash, Robertson, and Ford. The latter two are waiting with big smiles on their faces. They each have four geese. Ford has been coaching Bill. These are his first geese ever. Robertson is the most talkative man I've ever hunted with, but as he loads his geese in and helps with the others, a strange aura of silence has fallen over him. Like his little two-year-old boy, Jesse, he just grins a lot as though the world has come to honour him.

Nash is a mile in again, and I have to go and get him in the dark. The more the mud balls up around my boots, the more tired I get. It's dark out now, but at least the rain is gone and the stars are out. We meet on the road where Nash has been listening to the geese. He has long since given up shooting. The flocks are pretty much all back on their water. Nash has been counting strings of geese. He figures there may be as many as fifteen thousand in a slough of scarcely more than a dozen acres. Goose shit surrounds the slough like cigarette butts at a race track. And the sound is incredible: falsetto cackling, like a convention of auctioneers. When I yell to Nash across the road, he can't even hear me.

That night in the bar we have a pizza supper. We're all sleepy, so the talk has hit the drowsy stage by the time we reach the presentations. Calder and Robertson present Carver and Ford with official Crocus tractor caps. Nash presents them with Wayne Gretzky tractor caps. I toss them each a bag of Saskatchewan books and deliver a little speech. The idea is, if one of their literary colleagues says, "What? Serious writing in Saskatchewan?" they are to respond either with violence or one of the above-mentioned books. Ford and Carver are visibly touched by these presentations but even more moved by their need for sleep. We all hit the sack before ten o'clock.

By this time Doris has done twelve geese and two ducks for us. They've all met her and been smitten. She sits in a shack in a ghost town and flies through our dreams. Not too long from now, we will read each other's stories or poems with Doris as the muse. All through the storm, I imagine, she is listening to the wind. All day long we've been lying in the mud or shooting off boxes of shells at the indifferent gods, unaware that the muse was waiting for us . . . Amused by the muse . . . abused by the muse . . . but none too clever to . . . refuse the muse? These things dribble from my lips as I fall asleep to the thunderous applause of Nash's adenoids.

SEPTEMBER 27

Five o'clock, still pitch black out. I knock on everyone's door. Carver makes coffee, but this time there are only a few crumpled two-day-old doughnuts for breakfast. Calder is going to give it one more go. He heads out in the truck with Nash and Robertson. Ford and Carver come with me. Ford managed to bring down five geese, and he feels Carver should try his gun. Richard has generously decided to sit this one out. Neither Carver nor I have managed to bring down a goose, and Ford is eager that we do well this time. We drive out to the gravel road; the others return to the mud road. The stars are out and the dawn tilts slowly like a warm cup of tea. There is not a trace of a cloud. Ford coaches Carver on the handling of his gun and leaves in my car to pick up our plucked birds. Just as I'm settling into the ditch behind a telephone pole, the first wave comes over Carver's head two hundred yards down the road. He fires twice and two geese fall. One is only winged and takes off across the field flapping frantically over the swath. Carver leaps out of the ditch and gives chase. I race over to help him—after all, he has become one of the walking wounded—but Carver has suddenly regained his youthful legs. When I get there he sports two large specklebellies and an enormous grin. "Boy, isn't that something," he says.

We hurry back to our separate positions in the ditch, and over they come again. Carver knocks another goose down, this time a young Canada. A pair of specklebellies come at me from the sunrise, just in range. I stand up so that my body is shielded by the old telephone pole, lead the bird on the left, and fire. It seems to stop in mid-air and climb straight up. I fire again and down it comes, my first goose in four years. Carver waves. Minutes later a large chevron of honkers passes over our heads out of range, then another flock, this time lower. Carver fires first, knocks one down, and then I fire and down comes my first lesser

Canada. We chase our birds into opposite fields, bag them and lurch back into the ditch. It's about nine-thirty, the sun is climbing and hangs in a blue sky over a stubble field filled with thousands of specklebellies, Canadas, and snow geese. The geese tend to feed with their own kind, and so the snow geese stand out among the darker specimens in blotches of white. Thousands of geese are still in the slough to our west, and all day they will cross in waves of a hundred or more from slough to stubble, from stubble to slough. They fly high now, and Ray and I are extremely visible. What the hell.

Ford returns in my car, and with our instinct for show biz still proclaiming itself, we manage to meet him carrying our geese. He is ecstatic. He wants to shake our hands but of course they are filled with goosenecks.

"Oh boy!" he yells to Carver. "You liked it?" he asks, pointing to his gun. That one gun has accounted for nine geese so far this trip. "And you shot two of these?" he says to me. "You got two geese?"

I say, "Aw."

The six of us have brunch in Crocus and gas up for the long ride home. The woman at the pump asks us how we did and we tell her twenty geese, two ducks. The weather has been so bad that hardly anyone else has been able to get to where the geese are. The woman at the pumps tells us another group of five hunters picked up six geese, but we apparently were the only ones to do half-decently. This for me is a source of enormous pride. I'll be telling this story for a long time to come. The sleet will become snow, eventually a blizzard; the edge of a hurricane will become the eye of a hurricane; the bag will grow from twenty-two to forty-four; Carver's cuts on his left hand will become an ugly gash on his left arm . . .

"Doris took care of yiz, did she?" says the young woman at the pump.

"Yep," says Calder.

"Oh, the hunters really appreciate Doris," she goes on.

Calder's ears perk up. All of our ears perk up.

"Oh, Doris really pulls in some extra money in huntin

season," says the woman with all the innuendo she can muster.
"No kiddin," says Robertson.

I can see a poem flapping across the ditch as Robertson gets
back into the truck: "The Gooseplucker's Daughter" by William
B. Robertson. How will Carver handle this one? Will Ford beat
him to the punch? Will I?

"There's a dance on tonight," says the woman. "You guys
should come along."

"We have planes to catch," says Nash.

"Too bad," she sings. "Doris'll be there."

Carver has a coffee and cigarette at the Crocus Hotel café while
the other guys get their gear together. He's in his reading duds
again, surprisingly dapper: a beige raincoat he bought in London, brown turtleneck and tweed jacket, civilized shoes and
slacks that seem out of place in Crocus. He looks pleasantly
tired, a lot like that author whose pictures are on his dust jackets.

"You look like Raymond Carver," I tell him.

I can now confess to him that Jake had phoned just before his
reading to cancel the trip. He likes that: the fact that we risked
our hides against strong odds to come down here and be boys
again.

For most of us, I dare say, the trip amounted to an adventure
of nonheroic proportions. It was six guys wallowing in the mud
and struggling with other things as well: Carver with physical
pain, Ford with the unusual cold, Calder with his feelings about
killing things, Robertson with his old/new gun, and on it goes.
It was six guys unaccustomed to mud and hurricanes trying
(metaphorically at least) to shoot pigeons in the dark. Above all,
trying to help each other get through the day. Ford coached
Robertson in the duck blind; Nash and Carver bolstered my
courage when it looked bad for the trip; Calder wired on a
muffler by lying under his truck in a mud puddle so we could all
go in the first place; I ran around being host for several days and
worried for everyone; Carver made something like twenty cups
of coffee from his tiny pot at 5 A.M.

At the airport, Carver tries to thank me for a great hunt and gets choked up. I try to tell him that such rewards are his due because he happens to write well, but my words come stumbling out for want of sleep. Carver and Ford both want to come back and stay longer. We're already dreaming of next fall when great cackling legions of geese in flocks as wide as Saskatoon will once more descend from the North to fatten up on the grain fields, reminding us (who shoot at clay pigeons in the dark) that we were once Lee Henchbaw and we are from Sass-katchewan.

Spring in the Hub of Saskatchewan

*I*N MARCH, AFTER A MELT, there is a smell of thawing mud. The ice under your boots feels exhausted and gives way to slush. You go for puddlewalks in your wellies among the potholes on the streets. This is not spring. This is only Promise of Spring, a flirtatious spirit who inspires passions it has no intentions of satisfying. The next day you get a blizzard or a week of ten below. The geese know this and remain tourists somewhere south of the border.

Some say spring means pussywillows, or spring rain or crocuses. But here in Saskatoon I think about that day in April when the wind goes from harbinger to sandblaster. True spring in Saskatchewan comes with dust up your snoot and grit in your teeth. And out on the prairie that smell of earth and barnyards. Only then do the crows return to reclaim their trees, the gulls to preside over the town dump, and the geese pass over the houses in wedge after cackling wedge.

This Shot

*T*HE PHOTOGRAPHER HAD ASSEMBLED HIS EQUIPMENT in a neat pile on the front veranda. He straightened his jacket, touched the brim of his boater, swallowed what remained of his peppermint, and knocked. A young lady opened the door. She was tall, about eighteen. She leaned out from the door-frame looking down on him and then past him.

"Is that your tin lizzie?" she said.

"Yes," he said.

His Model T was parked on the street in front of the house. It had A.J. *Twill Photographer* in gold letters on the door. He had bought the car in 1923 from his uncle, and it still looked brand new.

The young lady reversed her grip on the doorframe and swung backwards into the house. She yelled, "Mah-ther?"

Mr. Twill thanked her and smiled, for after all wasn't it a beautiful morning, and didn't he have the most wonderful business in all of Saskatoon?

"You may as well come in," she said, neither surly nor encouraging. "My mum takes half her lifetime to get dressed in the morning."

When Mr. Twill (his friends called him Arthur) had brought his equipment into the front hall, the young lady was gone. He took off his boater, popped another peppermint into his mouth, and waited there in the dim light. Presently he spied another young lady backing her way out of the kitchen. She was dragging her little brother by the arms. She lugged him over to Mr. Twill and planted him there before him. And my, what a winsome creature she was.

"Hi," she said. "I'm Jennie and this is Burt."

"Arthur Twill," he tried to say, but his peppermint popped out of his mouth and bounced along the hardwood floor. Jennie's little brother seemed to think that this was hilarious, and he let fly with a very excessive laugh.

"Give me your hanky, Burt," said his sister.

"Blewaugh," said Burt, but after a small scene, he gave Jennie his hanky, which was probably dirty anyway. Jennie stooped down, plucked the peppermint off the floor, and told little Burt just to settle down. At least one of the (he pulled a work order from his pants pocket and glanced at the name) Mullens, yes, at least one of the Mullens had good manners.

The older sister reappeared with a sweater thrown over her shoulders. She gave young Jennie a look of appraisal and made a snuffling sound with her nose that sounded to Arthur like disapproval. The older sister looked up at the ceiling, baring her throat almost brazenly to the feeble light from the lamp in the hallway, and again yelled, "Mah-ther!"

"This is Peggy," young Jennie said, and she maintained a grip on little Burt's shoulders while Burt stared down at the photographer's shoes.

"Who said you could wear my scarf?" said Peggy.

"Burt," said Jennie, "you go get Dad. He's in the basement. And come right back, okay? Promise?"

Burt shook his head.

"And if you let that dog in here again, I will have your head. Do you hear me?"

Again little Burt shook his head. Jennie sighed for Mr. Twill's benefit and released the boy.

"Besides," Peggy purred, "it doesn't go with that blouse."

Jennie stuck out her tongue in Peggy's direction, crossed her arms, and leaned beside a large Canada goose, one of two mounted on the newel posts like sentinels at the foot of the stairway. Neither of the sisters spoke. Peggy sat on the stairs and began to arrange her skirt with such care that Mr. Twill seemed to have been forgotten.

"Well, well," he said, "it certainly is a fine day for taking pictures."

"I think we should take them all in the morgue," said Peggy.

"The morgue?" said Arthur Twill.

"She means the parlour," said Jennie. "She thinks dead animals are just swell."

"Dead animals in your parlour?" said the photographer. "May I see?" But before Mr. Twill could follow Peggy out of the front hall, her mother came to the head of the stairs.

"You must be the photographer," she cried. "Mercy me, why didn't anyone call me?"

"Your daughter was about to show me some—"

"Not in the morgue. Please, Peggy," said Florence Mullen, "and that's final." She turned to Jennie with a fearful little smile. "Where do you suppose your father has gotten to?"

"In the basement banging on things."

"And where is Burt? Jennie?"

"Fetching Dad."

As if on cue, Burt banged through the door from the kitchen. "Dad says he never knew nothin' about no photo graphy today."

"Never knew *anything*," said Jennie.

"Jennie, would you kindly inform your father he is wanted up here?" said Mrs. Mullen. "I'm afraid Mr. Twill will think badly of us. Lord help us, he might think we're this poorly organized all the time."

"Certainly not," said Mr. Twill with a winning smile. "Why, young Jennie was just intro intro introd—"

A large black dog had waddled into the hall, and it came straight for Mr. Twill. He stuck his nose into Mr. Twill's crotch, did some sniffing thereabouts, and licked him on the thigh. It all happened so fast poor Mr. Twill had scarcely any time to defend himself or his equipment. "Oh dear," he said dropping his hat on the floor. Now the animal was licking the leather on his camera and little Burt started laughing again.

Jennie appeared at the door. "Teck!" she cried, and the big dog slunk to her side. She grabbed the dog by the scruff of his neck and hustled him out the door. Fortunately there was no damage done.

"Teck? My, that's an unusual name for a dog," said Mr. Twill.

"He got his name from the school," said little Burt. These were his first words since Mr. Twill had arrived.

"From the school?" said Mr. Twill.

"Yeah," said Burt. "Teck."

"The technical school down by the bridge," said Peggy.

"Teck," said little Burt. "Like Teck? Don'tcha get it?"

"I get it," said Mr. Twill.

By and by Mr. Mullen sauntered in. He seemed a bit lost at first, and stopped at the door to clean his spectacles. He smiled at Mr. Twill and shook his hand. "It's nice to meet a fellow Arthur," Mr. Mullen said. "We're a small select fraternity here in Saskatoon."

Mr. Twill heartily agreed. He complimented Artie on his many fine hides and trophy heads. "I do my hunting with this," he said, pointing to his camera.

"At least you bring 'em back alive," said Artie, and the men chuckled.

"Artie," said Mrs. Mullen, "I hope you do not intend on having your picture taken in that old cardigan."

"What?"

"Your cardigan. Your *cardigan*."

"What's wrong with my cardigan?" asked Mr. Mullen.

"What's wrong with it? Just look at it. There's holes in the elbows and you've lost a button there. People will think I can't even sew."

"Florence, I don't intend to pose for no picture with my elbows showing."

"Artie," said Mrs. Mullen, "I *really wish* you would change out of that sweater."

"Know what?" said Burt. He was standing so close to Mr. Twill he had to look straight up. "I know somethin', I know a pome?"

"That's very nice, Burt," said Mr. Twill.

"Wanna hear? It's got a Arthur in it."

"All right," said Mr. Twill, "let's hear your poem."

"Burt," said Jennie, pointing her finger at him.

"This is just a pome I learnt at school," he said. In a very loud voice he began to recite. "Gene Gene made a machine, Joe Joe made it go, Art Art blew a fart and blew the bloody thing apart. Hahahahahahahahahahaha!"

Squealing like a pig, little Burt was lead by his ear from the living room. "Jennie, you're hurting him," said Peggy. She was smiling for the first time since Mr. Twill's arrival.

At last Mr. Twill had set up his equipment, Mrs. Mullen had prevailed upon her husband to change his clothes, and little Burt was allowed to return to the living room. Jennie held him in a firm grip. He shoved out his lower lip like a second tongue and stared at the floor. By now Jennie was flushed from her exertions with the dog and with little Burt and all.

"I think we'll sit here," said Mrs. Mullen. She acted as though she were hosting a grand party. "Burt? Jennie? Peggy? Where's Peggy? Artie?" she called to her husband, who was still out of the room. "You bring that girl downstairs, do you hear?"

At last the five Mullens assembled in the living room by the fireplace beneath the head of what had been a very large moose. Mr. Mullen thought it might be a good idea to include the moose in the pictures, but his wife thought otherwise. So the three young people sat on the sofa with little Burt flanked by his sisters, and Mr. and Mrs. Mullen stood behind them. On the first take, little Burt was startled by the flash of the powder.

"I wisht I could have one of them things," he said to his father.

"One of *those* things," said Jennie.

"What does that boy want?" said Mr. Mullen to Peggy.

"He wants a flash," said Peggy.

"A what?"

"He said he wants a *flash*," Peggy said again.

"Well why doesn't he just say so?" said Mr. Mullen.

Young Burt was so fascinated with the flash powder that he behaved himself and didn't sulk for the rest of the session. Mr. and Mrs. Mullen both smiled brightly, and Jennie of course, but nothing in the world, not even Mr. Twill's little dicky bird, would make Peggy smile. Such a shame it was, and such a pretty face!

When it was all over, young Jennie saw Mr. Twill to the door. She walked him out to his car and helped him put his equipment in the rumble seat. He wanted to express his appreciation to her for being so helpful, but he couldn't think of anything to say. Just as he was about to drive off, she called to him that he had forgotten his sample album. And when he had taken the album from her, placed it on the seat and taken the wheel again, she called once again because he had also forgotten his boater. She handed him the hat with a lovely smile.

"Why don't you wear your hat in the car?" she asked him, for he had placed the boater on top of the album.

"Oh," he said to Jennie. "Sometimes I do and sometimes I don't."

I was born fifteen years after this session. The above scene is of course partly my own invention, but as they say in the news business, I have some hard facts. I am Jennie's son and the nephew of Peggy and little Burt. I have the only photo that survived the above session. Its date is May 2, 1925. This shot is the only one I have ever found of my mother's family all together. The five Mullens of Saskatoon.

Aunt Peggy claims to remember the session in all of its salient details. For one thing, she insists that Mr. Twill became so infatuated with my mother, then only fifteen, that he urged her to come down to his studio so that he could shoot her alone. Apparently she turned down these and other offers. My mother claims not to remember this subplot.

And no, Mr. Twill did not become my father. According to the Saskatoon *Henderson's Directory*, Mr. Twill left town only two years later in 1927. It seems he succeeded in doing what the Mullens have always tried to do: disappear. Almost all of the family photos and memorabilia went up in the flames of my grandmother's stove some time in the late 1940s.

My Uncle Burt remembers the above session in much less detail. When I asked him why he looked so chipper, he says,

"Beats me." Was it his discovery of the wonders of flash powder, as Peggy always claims? "No," says Burt, as though this theory is too absurd for serious consideration.

My mother scarcely remembers anything about the picture. She hardly ever talks about those early years. She fields questions about her family from a certain distance; a careful reserve creeps into her voice, as though life among the Mullens was not the stuff of blissful memories. Her father was a bad provider and deaf to all conversation that was not about hunting and fishing. Her mother was too neurotic for motherhood or marriage. Her sister Peggy had what people in those days called a *reputation*. Her brother Burt was too young to be a kindred spirit.

The Mullens could rise to certain occasions and put on a cheerful united front, like throwing a party or sitting for photographs. But before and after the shot, where life is really lived, they endured family life like a judgement upon them.

Aunt Peggy is the only one in her family to have preserved any photos, and I've inherited most of them. Five or six of these are just of Peggy. They were taken when she was between the ages of sixteen and about forty-five. Unlike Florence, her mother, whose smile was her umbrella, her rod and her staff, Peggy would sooner die than smile for a photograph. And so in all of them she stares right at the camera with candour and world weariness, sometimes frowning but more often with a look of indulgent boredom as though, for her, the next moment is going to be a lot more interesting than this one. The older she gets in these shots, the more she comes to resemble the actress Joan Crawford.

More than once I mentioned this resemblance to Uncle Burt, and he used to frown with contempt at the very suggestion. Peggy's odyssey to Hollywood was always a sore point with the family.

I used to visit Uncle Burt in a care home out in the Saskatoon suburbs. In his final years he was suffering from Alzheimer's. At first he could shuffle all the way to the river with me. Sometimes we would walk along the path above the river bank and gaze at the pelicans and Canada geese that nest there in the summer.

He grew up by this river and hunted geese like these with his father in the thirties and forties. I used to imagine walking with him all the way upstream, six or seven miles along the South Saskatchewan, and right into town. We would march up to the house where my mother, Aunt Peggy, and Burt grew up. This house is only two blocks from the river. The street is lined with elm trees so big the branches reach out over the roadway and meet in the middle. The only dangers I ever heard of in that neighbourhood were the Steinbrecker boys and their unruly dogs, and since the boys were rebels at heart, my Aunt Peggy was their friend as often as their enemy.

Mom's, Peggy's, and Burt's house is a bulky two-storey wood frame with a big front veranda. This veranda is where, as teenagers, the two sisters would greet the boys who dropped in on them. There were many of these, even my mother will admit. At the front door the young men would take off their caps (later, fedoras and boaters) and spin them like horseshoes onto the antlers that sprouted from the walls of the front hall and the living room. Others would aim for the big Canada geese that were mounted on the newel posts at the foot of the staircase. If my mother ever had any use for the past she might write a memoir of this lively time. And if she did, the front cover could feature a stuffed goose wearing a cloth cap.

The piano stood beneath a huge moosehead in the living room. I wonder if it looked out of place there, surrounded by all the evidence of the hunt: the gamebirds, the bear hide, and the deer and elk peering glassy-eyed from their mountings. This is where the young people would gather to sing with Florence Mullen at the keyboard. Peggy's favourite was "That's Peggy O'Neil," because of the name. My mother and Peggy learned to Charleston in that same living room, and when things really got going, the dancers would spill out into the hall and dance around the kitchen. My mother preferred the dancing to anything else in those days, and her father always said her brains were in her feet.

When I was a little boy, our family inherited Florence's piano, a modest upright little Everett with a crazed finish. I am sorry to report that no one in our house ever did that piano much justice.

My mother's old house is now dwarfed by highrise apartments and office buildings on the fringe of downtown Saskatoon. It looks besieged. Any day now the house could fall to the wrecker's ball. This bothers me. Sometimes I imagine going inside with no one around. I would spend my time snooping for clues. Perhaps I would find some animal hair, or a pheasant's tailfeather in the basement, or the crushed skeleton of a chinchilla in the back yard. Perhaps I would hear my mother's long-dead mother playing the piano and singing "That's Peggy O'Neil."

When I was a boy our family visited Saskatoon and the Mullen house several times. I have a memory of feeble light from the street, darkish oak trim in the rooms downstairs, and everywhere the threadbare signs of a former gentility that must have been their style in long-ago Ontario. I remember Granddad Mullen's big high hunting boots next to Granny Mullen's delicate suede snowboots. And guns: shotguns, hunting rifles with walnut stocks, the same brown as the oak doorframes. Old camping gear stowed here and there, fishing rods, blackened pots, binoculars. All of this piled on sleeping bags and canvas, as though the men are always just back from a camping trip or always just about to leave.

My mother remembers the house in terms of the critters they kept. To hear her and Aunt Peggy tell it, they had more animals than Noah's ark. Just a preliminary list would include Teck, their Labrador, and the exotic fowl and pedigreed hens Grandfather Mullen would buy from time to time to win ribbons with or perhaps make a fortune. These he lodged in the garage. My mother was sickly as a child, and for years they kept a Jersey cow tethered in the back yard. I used to ask why. More than once I was told it was because, as a child, my mother needed the cream. But surely they could have had their cream delivered by the milkman like anyone else in Saskatoon. Once my mother turned to me and said, "A cow in our *backyard*? Whatever for?"

But Peggy remembers the cow, and Mom's uncertain health is a part of family lore that she never denies. She must have had good powers of recuperation, because according to all sources, she grappled with and defeated the fatal flu of 1918, and a year or two later, polio. More than once I have asked her how her own mother coped with all these maladies. And more than once she has told me that she didn't really have a mother. "I had to be my own mother," she says.

Her mother, my granny Mullen, nee Florence Sloan, was born into money. She was sent off to a finishing school where she studied piano, needlepoint, elocution and other such fineries, and where she was to remain until she was of marriageable age. Under no circumstances was she to work. At anything. No girlie ever needed money, her father told her. In this picture of the five Mullens she smiles bravely.

Her husband smiles mischievously. My hunting grandfather. Like Granny Mullen, he was Ontario Irish, a lapsed Catholic. Artie Mullen loved dogs, boats, guns, fishing gear, anything that kept him in or near the water. Artie and Florence met on a beach near Lindsay, Ontario, where she was making her social debut. The first time he saw her, he was standing barelegged in the water doing repairs on a canoe. She stood on the wharf nearby. In the course of their conversation she informed him that she was giving a piano recital at the Literary that night. As the story is told, it was the first time Artie Mullen had ever come willingly out of the water. He put on his best suit and attended her recital, and promptly fell in love.

Florence's father refused to attend the wedding. Florence's dowry were her piano and clothes. Artie brought his tools, his guns, his fishing rods and boat, his skinning knives and meat saws. Everything but the smokehouse, they used to say. For some reason they decided to go west. Some say Artie had notions of being a gentleman farmer, some say he wanted to escape the long and disapproving shadow of Florence's father, and some say Artie simply wanted to go where the hunting and fishing were better. No one seems to know where Florence stood in all of this, but I can guess.

In spite of her father's angry dismissal of her, in spite of the financial embarrassment she had to endure in Saskatchewan, she remained devoted to her father long after he died. The farther away in space and time, the more she revered him. When she was an old woman and I was her little confidant, she told me *I never should have left him.*

According to Peggy her mother wept a long stream the night of her wedding and wept rivers all through the honeymoon because she missed her father so. Both daughters agree that Florence hated intimacy of any kind, and never once did a sign of tenderness pass between Florence and Artie. She should never have married, Peggy would say. She should have gone with her piano onto the concert stage. My mother claims to remember none of this, but several times I have caught her wondering out loud how her parents ever managed to have three children.

No girlie ever needed money, her father would repeat, but the old patriarch was probably not thinking of Artie Mullen. Nor, I suspect, was he thinking very clearly about his own daughter. To Florence, keeping track of accounts was a bother. Artie was worse. He was a life-long devotee to get-rich-quick schemes. He gave away thousands to grubstake prospectors on promises of a quick strike. When he gave up on farming he turned to insurance and formed a small company in Saskatoon. But he was better at minding the lakes and woods than minding his own shop, and through the years one of his partners managed to siphon off enough funds to bankrupt the firm. By the time my mother was eighteen or nineteen, the family was penniless. Artie Mullen was not destined to be a breadwinner.

Perhaps old Moneybags Sloan did what he could to keep the family afloat. There must have been a partial reconciliation of some sort, because he came west on occasion to see how his daughter was faring. He was a hit with little Burt, and my mother and Peggy found him amusing, if only for his stately, well-bred Irish accent and his lordly bearing at the supper table. If one of the children misbehaved he would intone, *The black pig is on your back.*

Peggy is no more reticent about recounting the past than she was about any other form of pleasure. She is my main source for all of this, a writer's dream come true: black sheep and irrepressible gossip. Peggy was the oldest and the rebel in the family. She saw domestic rules and table manners as mere challenges to her own ingenuity. When Peggy misbehaved at the supper table, Old Man Sloan consigned her to the parlour where she had to sit facing a corner in the darkened room. Thus, the parlour and the pig became Peggy's.

Along the walls of the parlour where other houses would display bookshelves or knickknacks Artie Mullen displayed his guns, including an old Colt .45 that Peggy had somehow learned to load during her disconsolate bouts with the pig. Perhaps Peggy dreamed of saving her family from robbers or perhaps she had plans to scare the Steinbrecker boys and their nasty dogs down the street. The parlour was surrounded on three sides with glass cases crowded with mounted gamebirds, rodents, pets, and varmints trapped and skinned by Artie and little Burt. It was Granny Mullen who christened their parlour "the morgue."

Her only defence in a household given over to the pleasures of the sporting life was for two decades to feign sickness. Whenever any crisis arose (a fight with Peggy or a bill collector or the first appearance of a daughter's menstrual blood), Florence would take to her bed. She was available to play the piano at the drop of a hat, but whenever reality began to impinge, "Mother is not herself today." And so my mother became her own mother and everyone else's too, a self-appointed Cinderella in a house as feckless and gay and eccentric as a talking movie. And sister Peggy became something else entirely. She never learned to cook, she never married, she took as many lovers as she pleased, and frequently intent upon her own misery, she never smiled for a camera.

When she was a teenager she would duck out of her chores, so my mother had to get supper and wash the dishes and take care of little Burt. Sometimes at night Peggy would wait till the house was quiet and slip out of bed. My mother would wake up and see her climbing out the window. Peggy would swear her to secrecy and my mother would have to endure the tension that gathered in her stomach, which was always the preliminary to another scene between Peggy and her mother. To my mother's dread, Peggy would slide from the second-storey window onto the back porch roof, then drop to the ground to meet one of the local pariahs with a bottle of home brew and a bad reputation.

In the spring of 1924, a year before Mr. Twill came along with his boater and his camera, when Peggy was sixteen, the black pig must have become a permanent fixture on her back. I am referring here to her involvement with the chinchillas, one of my grandfather's many ill-fated get-rich schemes. Sometimes it was prospectors, sometimes it was gadgets Artie would invent and try to sell, and sometimes it involved breeding animals in the garage at the back of their lot. In the spring of 1924, it was chinchillas. Artie had a plan to raise thousands of these rodents, slaughter them, skin them, and sell the little hides for what furriers in those days called Chinese mink. Perhaps my grandfather envisioned bevies of fashionable but purse-conscious ladies wearing coats from his own garage.

As usual he enlisted the help of his daughters, and as she always did, Peggy fell in love with the unfortunate animals. Never known to be patient with children, Peggy was a sucker where animals were concerned. The chinchillas were not smelly rodents to her; they were specially small short-eared rabbits and therefore even cuter than rabbits. They were squealy and cuddly and completely dependent upon their captors for food. Artie Mullen's chinchillas were the ultimate underdog, and underdogs of all description were Aunt Peggy's bailiwick.

On that warm spring morning, Peggy awoke to the sound of squealing. It sounded to her like crying from a ward of aroused newborn infants. She leapt out of bed. She raced down the stairs and grabbed the Colt .45 from the wall of the parlour. She dashed outside in her nightie and bare feet and threw open the garage door.

The Steinbrecker dogs looked up from their carnage. Not one chinchilla had survived the attack. These were big dogs, though I don't know what kind, and there must have been several. They looked at Peggy, perhaps wondering as dogs must what she was going to do. She opened up on them. She claims to have missed every one, but I have my doubts. The dogs vaulted out of the garage and down the lane with Peggy not far behind and still shooting until she found herself with an empty revolver swearing a blue streak in front of the Steinbreckers' home.

She looked down the street and saw a group of men with lunch pails on their way to work. The men had come to a sudden halt. Peggy adjusted her nightie, flung her hair over her shoulder, and walked back into the house.

Right now my Aunt Peggy lies in a hospital bed suffering from lung fibroids and a recent stroke. She cannot return to her apartment in the old heart of Winnipeg. She must lie on her back and wait until a room in a nursing home becomes available, and I dare say she is visiting the past that my mother has no use for a great deal these days. Whenever I can, I come to Winnipeg to see her, but Winnipeg is a long way from Saskatoon.

My mother swears she doesn't remember the story about the routing of the Steinbreckers' dogs, that it's just another of her sister's wild fabrications. But once on a walk with Uncle Burt, the Alzheimer haze seemed to lift from his pale blue eyes, and he said, "That Peggy. She sure drove those dogs out. She showed 'em. She couldn't shoot worth a hoot, but by the Jesus she must of nicked one or two." And then, as though to verify his brief return to my world, he pointed at me and smiled and said my name. "Dave."

The smile is Granny Mullen's. As I mentioned, she was particularly big on smiles. They were exacted like tithes whenever her daddy visited the house in Saskatoon. Perhaps Florence believed that smiles could hide any number of hideous uncertainties that reality imposes on a family, but Peggy, with her self-inflicted Joan Crawford complex, would always be there to counter her mother's relentless innocence with a worldly frown. And now, as Peggy lies face down in a bed in the Misericordia Hospital while the life of Winnipeg drives off without her, and with the dull fibroid pain upon her lungs, she might indeed wonder if the black pig hasn't returned to sit on her back.

I'm writing this memoir as a charm or a prayer for my prodigal aunt and my eighty-three-year-old mother, the last of the Mullens. Before their picture was taken by Mr. Twill, they moved through their days in Saskatoon as I do now. And after Mr. Twill had taken his shot and driven away with the immortal credo that still brings a smile to Mom and Peggy's lips, *Sometimes I do and sometimes I don't*, the five Mullens carried on their secret lives unwitnessed and soon to be forgotten. Even their house is about to be forgotten.

A good memoir is worth a thousand photographs; it struggles to release the captives in the frame. But I wasn't even there to witness the lives of the Mullens before they faded from the picture. So here I am now, seven decades later, taking my best shot. Sometimes when I walk past the old house on a summer night I can almost hear my grandmother singing *That's Peggy O'Neil* . . . Sometimes I think I can write the black pig off Peggy's back. Sometimes I think I can give my mother a memory or at least a reason for remembering. Sometimes I do and sometimes I don't.

Hoovering to Byzantium

FOR A LONG TIME I'VE BEEN LOOKING for an all-purpose verb that describes what writers do when they use (lift? recycle? borrow? deconstruct? steal? rework? draw from?) someone else's story to tell their own. Take the case of Herodotus. He is very popular these days. More than twenty-four centuries have passed since he recounted the story of Gyges and Candaules, but this story still beckons modern writers to the keyhole of a certain ill-fated bedroom. Candaules, King of Lydia, has conceived an immoderate heat for his queen. She is never named, but she is the most powerful character in the story. The irrepressible king doesn't seem to realize this. He brags to his friend Gyges (body-guard and confidant) that the queen's beauty is unsurpassed. He insists that Gyges hide in their bedroom and see for himself. Gyges declines the offer. It is improper, he argues, but the king insists. Under orders Gyges hides in the royal boudoir. He spies the queen naked, then steals from the room. The next day he is summoned by the queen, who spotted him slinking out of the boudoir. She is outraged by her husband's indecency. She gives Gyges an ultimatum: either he die for this act of voyeurism or kill the author of it and marry her. Once again, Gyges protests against any involvement, and once again to no avail. He agrees to serve the queen, murders Candaules, and rules by her side in Lydia.

Modern writers as different from one another as Mario Vargas Llosa and Michael Ondaatje have revived (revived?) the Gyges and Candaules story in various ways. Here is an interesting example from another contemporary novelist. The story is about a middle-aged man of reasonable affluence who has yet to learn the fundamentals of love. He is a historian of sorts, but at this difficult time in his life he discovers he would rather read myths than history. One of his favourite stories is that of Gyges and Candaules. In fact, it turns into a real life scenario when he is given the opportunity to play Gyges, destroy the king, and leap into bed with the queen.

Our man meets a fascinating, learned, intuitive woman whom he considers to be ugly and obnoxious. She has an irritating habit of lecturing him. He believes her to be interfering with his private concerns, and in some mysterious sense he sees her as a devil, perhaps even *the* Devil. They argue and eventually have a fight. A physical fight. He wins by beating her in the face, but for both of them, this brawl is the beginning of love.

His ordeal is far from over. He has to confront his best friend, the Candaules figure, and humiliate him so severely that the two can never be friends again. This revenge (described as "eating up" the other fellow) involves forcing him to see his own duplicity.

By now some of you will have guessed which novel I am summarizing. In case not, I can provide a final clue. The symbol that draws together the separate threads of this story is a severed head believed to utter prophecies that lead to strange and forbidden knowledge. Its voice is that of the demonic woman, who has an uncanny grasp of our hero's deeper self.

Many readers of contemporary British fiction will have guessed that this novel is *A Severed Head* (1961) by Iris Murdoch, the story of Martin Lynch-Gibbon and his bewildering love for Honor Klein. Well done, except it is *also* a summary from the plot of *Fifth Business* (1970) by the Canadian novelist Robertson Davies. Virtually every detail of my summary fits both novels. More than a decade ago I was jolted by my discovery of these similarities. Hmm, says the young scholar, eyebrows raised, moral judgements in their silos at the ready. *Hmm. This bears looking into.*

I was living in Toronto, finishing my first book of fiction (*Jokes for the Apocalypse*). It was late in the winter of 1983, and I was on a very long leave from university teaching. I thought I could take a brief rest from the rigours of fiction writing to do an essay on the similarities between the two novels. *A Severed Head* was present in *Fifth Business* like a palimpsest. You just had to scrape a bit and there it was. I would first approach Davies and give him a chance to defend himself by phrasing my key question as diplomatically as possible: Is *Fifth Business* your response to *A Severed Head?* A decade ago such a question might be considered part of the new critical discourse. Among certain university writers *all* novels were responses or reactions to previous novels.

Early in 1984 I called Davies's secretary at Massey College and made an appointment to see him. He greeted me with warmth and consideration, and he answered my first few questions without difficulty.

"Is *Fifth Business* your response to Iris Murdoch's *A Severed Head?*" I said boldly.

"What do you mean?" he said.

I rattled off my list of similarities, which was not short, concluding with the way Davies uses the story of Gyges and Candaules, and he grew quiet. The temperature in the room seemed to drop.

"Well," he said at last, "you must realize, Mr. Carpenter, that many writers of the twentieth century like to use myths."

Until this moment his answers had been direct and thoughtful. This response seemed preposterously inadequate. Aha, I said to myself. Bull's-eye. I pushed my thesis further, but to no avail. Our conversation wandered into innocuous territory.

The more I thought about my interview with Davies, however, the less enthused I became over my planned essay. What was I going to say? That Davies the master novelist was a closet literary lifter? And what business did I, a young neophyte with more ego than reputation, have meddling with the reputation of a man I respect? I dropped the project and it died right there.

But I never forgot Davies's discomfort at my question—that it had been an invasion of some kind. To this day, I'm convinced that Robertson Davies read Iris Murdoch's *A Severed Head* before he wrote *Fifth Business* and found things in Murdoch's novel he could use in his own. (Readers will note that I have not used the P word.)

To be fair we also need to look at the differences between these two novels. Murdoch's is a modern comedy of manners for a sophisticated sixties audience with at least some familiarity with D.H. Lawrence and his "dark gods." Her story begins when Martin Lynch-Gibbon's marriage breaks down. His lovely wife, Antonia, is a fashionable society beauty five years Martin's senior. She tells him one day that she has fallen in love with her psychoanalyst, a charismatic American named Palmer Anderson who is Martin's best friend and our King Candaules figure. Until this moment, Martin has been drifting along in a complacent wooze of pleasure and comfort. He loves his mistress Georgie, sort of, but keeps her a secret from everyone. He also loves his wife, sort of. He is a wine merchant and he finds the business prosperous and fulfilling, sort of. But when wife Antonia tells him that she wants to leave him for Palmer Anderson, Martin promptly falls, however shallowly, in love with her. These three characters attempt to be civil about things. Martin outdoes himself as the good loser. "There was nothing I could do," he says, "except act out with dignity my appointed task of being rational and charitable." His wife tries to mother Martin through his agonies and maintains an almost daily connection with him. She persuades him to go and see her new lover, Palmer. Martin does, and the two men try to revitalize their friendship.

Enter Honor Klein, half-sister of Palmer, a Cambridge professor of anthropology and custodian of the "dark gods" of the aboriginal people she lectures about. It is dislike at first sight, but Honor and Martin are thrown together on a number of awkward occasions because Honor's brother and Martin's wife are now living together. They fight and, soon after, Martin acquires a fascination for the repellent and devilish woman. He is falling violently in love. Things have become very complicated indeed. Martin pursues the woman all the way back to her home in Cambridge, and under the influence of drink and eros, breaks into her boudoir when she is in bed with—are we ready for this?—her brother, the psychoanalyst, who was supposed to be with Martin's wife, Antonia.

The charismatic king has been exposed, so to speak. From this moment on, Anderson loses his power over Martin, Martin's hapless wife Antonia, and even over Anderson's half-sister and longtime lover, Honor Klein. Martin repels Anderson from his wife, regains her for a brief, quiet, boring reunion, but soon yearns to be with Honor. No longer does she seem ugly. He tells the woman of his hopeless passion for her. She tells him, "Because of what I am and because of what you saw I am a terrible object of fascination for you. I am a severed head such as primitive tribes and old alchemists used to use, anointing it with oil and putting a morsel of gold upon its tongue to make it utter prophesies. And who knows but that long acquaintance with a severed head might not lead to strange knowledge." She discourages Martin's advances and he backs away.

Just when Martin feels as though the two halves of his life might be coming together (the feeling and the thinking half), his wife Antonia delivers her second little surprise: she has always loved his brother Alexander, and wants a divorce so that she can marry *him*. Once again, Martin prepares himself for the loneliness and confusion of living alone, but this time without his mistress, Georgie, who is undergoing therapy with (you guessed it) Palmer Anderson. Reenter Honor Klein. She has decided not to turn her back on Martin. By the end of the novel they are about to embark on an adventure with one another that might just have something to do with love.

In summary this novel might sound like a soap opera for people with a B.A. in psychology, but it's wittier and more challenging than my summary has allowed. All six characters have gone through the convulsions of love and separation, and all six emerge from their chaos and futility with a new partner. Georgie flies off with Palmer to New York, the place Martin has never managed to take her. Antonia settles in with Alexander, whom she has always adored. And Martin and

Honor bring the novel to a close with a relationship that "has nothing to do with happiness, nothing whatever." Martin says to Honor, "I wonder if I shall survive it." She says with a smile, "You must take your chance!" And here are the last words of the novel: "I gave her back the bright light of the smile, now softening at last out of irony. 'So must you, my dear!'"

Irony is the operative word here. Much more than a diversion for the jejune at heart, Murdoch's novel is an ironic look at the breakdown of familiar patterns in the life of a middle-class man and the world he walks through without ever quite getting the goods on. Martin's world is filled with self-assured, articulate, well-educated people who dispense a great deal of advice, but almost always the advice is wrong or leads to chaos. Murdoch's characters live amid the plenty of the British postwar boom, but the one commodity they cannot seem to lay by is certainty. *A Severed Head* is a manual on how to survive without certainty. The novel enjoyed popular success and an afterlife when it was made into a film in 1970, the year *Fifth Business* was published.

Davies's novel was one of the first serious works of Canadian fiction to reach an international audience. Writers as various and eminent as John Fowles, Anthony Burgess, Saul Bellow, and John Irving have sung its praises in print. An impressive stack of scholarly articles has been published on *The Deptford Trilogy*, of which *Fifth Business* is the first and most illustrious instalment. It seems to draw very heavily on *A Severed Head* for some of its characters and subplots and for some of its themes and mythic structures, but the novel has a life of its own.

Fifth Business is the story of Dunstable Ramsay, perhaps the most famous curmudgeon in Canadian literature. His story begins when he is ten years old and has a disagreement with his friend, Percy Boyd Staunton. Dunstable refuses to fight Percy, and instead tries to ignore his bad-tempered taunts and snowballs. To avoid Percy's last salvo, he steps in front of a couple going for a walk. One is Reverend Amasa Dempster, the other his young pregnant wife, Mary. Percy's snowball (which has a stone inside) strikes Mary on the head with great force, and she falls to the ground. She is taken to the doctor where she gives birth prematurely to a grotesque unnaturally small child. For the rest of her life, Mary will be confined in one way or another. She will be stigmatized as the "simple" woman of Deptford.

Her assailant, Percy Boyd Staunton, is our Candaules figure here. He's the son of the richest man in Deptford. He manages to silence young Dunstable (a reluctant Gyges figure) with a threat, and Dunstable takes on the guilt of the entire tragedy. He devotes a good part of the next sixty years of his life to the care and maintenance of Mary Dempster whom he comes to see as a saint.

Paul Dempster, the tiny grotesque child of Mary, grows up to be a strange, inverted Christ figure. While still a boy he is seduced by the circus and runs away from home to become a performer and a master conjuror who creates miracles of illusion on stage. He changes his name to Magnus Eisengrim. Percy Boyd Staunton grows from a young son of a bitch to a very rich bastard, but he still maintains a connection, even perhaps a friendship, with Dunstable. He is so proud of his *queen* Leola's beauty that he insists upon showing nude photographs of her to Dunny/Gyges. (Just as Dunstable is a reluctant Gyges figure, Leola is a reluctant Queen of Lydia figure.) Percy Boyd Staunton changes his name to Boy Staunton, which is consistent with his self-image as an eternally young and fatally handsome swordsman among the ladies. Dunstable Ramsay grows up to be a school master of history, a hagiographer of world renown, and changes his name to Dunstan Ramsay, after St. Dunstan, who in saintly lore is said to have grabbed the Devil by the nose with a pair of tongs. He resists the role of Gyges or any other heroic role thrust upon him to become instead a sort of moral historian. Dunstan Ramsay is Fifth Business. He is "the odd man out, the person who has no opposite of the other sex. And you must have Fifth Business because he is the one [in an opera] who knows the secret of the hero's birth, or comes to the assistance of the heroine when she thinks all is lost, or keeps the hermitess in her cell, or may even be the cause of somebody's death if that is part of the plot. The prima donna and the tenor, the contralto and the basso, get all the best music and do all the spectacular things, but you cannot manage the plot without Fifth Business." The woman who tells Dunstan this is Lieselotte Vitzlipützli (Liesl for short), a Swiss gargoyle and personal devil for Dunny. Very much like Honor Klein in *A Severed Head*, Liesl becomes less loathsome to Dunny. Indeed, after she and Dunny fight, they make love. Liesl is the brains behind Magnus Eisengrim's magic show, the *Soirée of Illusions*. One of her functions with the magic show is to be the voice for the Brazen Head, a severed head that speaks prophesies and tells fortunes to the audience.

I have mentioned that *A Severed Head* is a comedy of manners about a society in disarray. Appearances are deceptive in the extreme. The gurus in Murdoch's novel are frequently wrong. Circumstances in Martin's world dictate a disengagement from anything resembling a traditional morality. Martin can try to do good, he can try to acknowledge his own guilt or judge others as guilty, he can try to see the many ways in which he too is culpable in this conspiracy of infidelity and counter-infidelity, but he must eventually pursue a quest for identity that leads away from the comforts of middle-class morality or any recognizable code of decency and move into the darkness of Honor Klein's neoprimitive vision of things. Whatever Martin gains, it will be at the cost of stability in his life.

By contrast, Dunstan Ramsay comes from a family and a small town that have none of the grace, affluence, and sophistication of Martin's world. Dunstan grows up under the shadow of Calvinism; if he can't feel enough guilt, he will manufacture it. When his gurus (like Liesl) teach him at last that his Calvinistic beliefs are more destructive than they are redeeming, he comes to espouse a Jungian vision of life with its timeless cycles and archetypal world of wonders, and this vision lends stability and a sort of poetry to his life. In *Fifth Business*, the gurus are usually wise and almost always right, and like Dunstan Ramsay, who is frequently lectured to by priests, philosophers, and learned women, we the readers are enticed toward this Jungian vision of things. Utterly unlike *A Severed Head*, *Fifth Business* is a masterpiece of didactic fiction, a learned polemic on the eternal verities by a devout Jungian. Indeed, there is enough theoretical discussion in Davies's novel to constitute a sort of Jungian gloss on Murdoch's. The difference is that Dunstan and Davies remain relentlessly moral in their outlook.

It starts with an accident. Or is it syncronicity? A small missile strikes a saintly, sensual, and allegedly "simple" woman on the head. The missile mysteriously disappears throughout most of the novel and then reappears. Our narrator spends the rest of his life trying to come to terms with this life-altering event, and from boyhood to manhood, he sees miracles that could belong in a history of the saints (for example, the miraculous appearance of a statue of Mary). From the favourite hangouts of his small town to the musty rooms of the private school where he teaches, haunted by religious miracles, he carries with him the secrets of the past. Perhaps the greatest secret has to do with the grotesque and tiny child whose parents are a sad parody of Mary and Joseph. But their child's life is a sort of miracle epic. Our narrator remains a bachelor in Toronto and courts the company of priests and theologues. He is inflexibly moral to the end.

I know, I'm repeating myself. But I'm *also* summarizing for you the plot of a more recent American novel, John Irving's *A Prayer for Owen Meany* (1989). All of these bizarre details fit Irving's novel. This time the saintly/sensual Mary figure dies in the accident, and she's more of a Magdalene than a Madonna. So is the mysterious statue that seems to preside over her memory. The missile is no longer a snowball with a piece of granite inside; it is now a baseball. (Irving's story is, after all, primarily an American novel.) But all in all, these and many other plot details are remarkably similar.

John Irving has made no secret of his admiration for Robertson Davies's *Fifth Business*. And he goes one step further. His schoolmaster narrator, John Wheelwright, reminds us that he has taught *Fifth Business* "with the greatest pleasure" to his literature class in a Toronto private school. "I consider Mr. Davies," Wheelwright tells one of his colleagues, "an author of such universal importance that I choose not to teach what is 'Canadian' about his books, but what is wonderful about them."

Perhaps something "wonderful" from Davies's novel survives in Irving's, something to do with the narration of miracles to an audience in need of them. But my speculation scarcely does justice to John Irving. For *Owen Meany* is utterly and unmistakably irvingated with his own concerns and obsessions, such as the war in Vietnam, and with the memory, the smell, the mythology of his New England setting. Speaking of New England mythology, note Irving's debt to Nathaniel Hawthorne. Both novels deal in saintly/sensual New England women who have a child out of wedlock because of a liaison with a minister whose cowardly lips are sealed. And both women are pretty fond of red and handy with the needle, as I recall.

I wonder if Robertson Davies could prevent himself from smiling at the above passage from *A Prayer for Owen Meany*; no doubt this is Irving's acknowledgement to Davies. I wonder if Davies could prevent himself from smiling at the entire novel. Surely imitation is the sincerest form of flattery. (And if so, perhaps Iris Murdoch and Herodotus are also smiling.)

I must admit, this essay is a bit more personal in its origins than I have so far admitted. I have a little confession to make. A few years after my meeting with Davies and after my own first book of fiction had come out, I was at a literature conference. A colleague of mine, David Williams, approached me. He had just read my book, *Jokes for the Apocalypse*.

"What's this Robertson Davies connection?" he said.

"What do you mean?" I asked.

He quoted a phrase to me: "the revenge of the unlived life."

I must have lost the same amount of colour as Robertson Davies did some years earlier. The phrase, spoken by my narrator Ham Walmsley, came originally from the mouth of—you guessed it—Liesl in *Fifth Business*.

Williams offered to extend his list of similarities, but I derailed him. I couldn't bear to hear it. I, David Carpenter, a "good lad" the neighbourhood mothers had said, a former boy scout, a regular attender at the local Sunday school, a man who had grown up believing that honesty was the best policy, I had taken . . . lifted . . . stolen . . . appropriated . . . I had . . . I had gone and p-p-p . . .

My embarrassment was the beginning of this essay. First of all, why was I embarrassed? Why did Davies become so diffident? Were we both getting protective of our lair, or were we wondering whether we held full title to it? Or better still, where do writers' notions of ownership of literary commodities come from? Where do our notions of originality and literary theft come from? I can begin to confront these questions by looking first at my own sense of culpability at having been discovered with my net in Robertson Davies's goldfish bowl.

What interests me here are the ways in which we writers deploy our reading in order to write our books. I have to approach this phenomenon not as a theorist or an academic sleuth, but as a writer. So many theorists and academics from Eliot to Foucault have made pronouncements on the ways in which literary discourse arises from a whole galaxy of literary discourse, that the long shadow of an orthodoxy has been cast over the subject. One is apt to forget the utterly personal, sometimes turbulent, even neurotic process by which a writer's words find their way onto the page. If we listen to theorists only, we might be tempted to think of the creative process as a self-possessed act of scholarship or an exercise in cleverness; or that the best literature is like a rising corporate executive, the literature with the best connections.

I want to begin with the state of mind that led up to my work on "Jokes for the Apocalypse," the title novella of my book. I began writing it in the summer of 1980 at a Canadian writers' colony in Fort San, Saskatchewan. We writers lived and worked in a huge, spooky old chalet in the Qu'Appelle Valley. This residence was filled (it seemed to all of us) with the ghosts of hundreds, perhaps thousands, of mustard gas victims from the first great war and many more victims of tuberculosis. Our chalet bore a physical resemblance to the one in Thomas Mann's *The Magic Mountain*, with its rows of screened-in porches for sitting in the cool dry air. Strange and memorable things happened to me in that chalet and to other writers who came there, year after year.

The place was frequented with ghostly memories and so was I. I was not thinking a great deal about literature or about Robertson Davies. As always, the words of my favourite books were no doubt hovering somewhere in my brain and even lodged in my tongue, but my mind at the time of composition was unusually feverish with the story I was about to write, peopled by characters who already had their own voice, which in turn emerged to some extent from some very personal details in my life. I was hungrily sucking up all sorts of things from life and memory. For one thing, I was uneasy over an affair I had had with a young woman. I couldn't be sure that I had acted responsibly. I was beginning to wonder whether I had ever acted responsibly. A sentence of Adele Wiseman's, a writer and friend of mine, kept circling around in my head: *How can men ever begin to understand the delicate ecology of those adoring young women? The men just haul on their woodsmen's boots and stomp around on the flowers.*

I began my story with an accurate memory of once picking up a hitchhiker. Soon the memory passed into fiction, and my main narrator lurched into his own identity, oozing alcohol from every pore. Ham Walmsley is long on charm and short on compassion, and his life is about to collapse. Just as I was on my way to Fort San when I picked up my entirely real hitchhiker, he too is on his way there. He is going to a job, teaching band to teenagers.

Walmsley is a charming man haunted by an emotionally desolate past. He has a curious relationship with guilt: he repels it and courts it with impressive ease. He has long, carefree lapses from the ordinary rules of consideration for others and then sudden attacks of guilt. The guilt is part of a cycle; it is so overwhelming that it guarantees and renews Ham's need for another binge. He has sex with his lovely young hitchhiker and then drops her off the next morning so that she can hitch back to the city they both came from. A terrible fate befalls her and Ham begins to feel responsible. Then he blocks her out so that he can no longer even remember what she looks like. But still he suffers terribly. Part of his atonement is to unburden himself to a colleague down at Fort San, an artist who is older than he, a woman named Lena Rotzoll with an adventurous past who has done her share of suffering. They exchange anguished accounts and for a while form a bond of fellow sufferers. When Ham Walmsley's atonement is in full swing, he is at last visited by Lola, his mysterious hitchhiker, who is either a ghostly memory or a memorable ghost. I could never be sure about the ghosts of Fort San (which is a book in itself); Ham Walmsley can never be sure if this last visitation from Lola is anything more than a desperate eruption from his own suppressed imagination.

His imagination has begun to turn on him and clamour for expression. Here is a rumination from near the beginning of "Jokes" in which Ham is thinking back about the dog he loved when he was a boy. His mother had finally had the dog put down. "I blew up . . . I yelled at her and she told me she knew I slept with that dog. The only reason she'd ever let it go on was that she felt sorry for me. It occurred to me years later what she was really accusing me of. Not that there would have been anything wrong with it. In the absence of love you start to wonder if *any* kind of love isn't perhaps its own justification . . . Such thoughts for a man who teaches band. *Revenge of the unlived life*" (italics mine).

Compare the above with the following passage from *Fifth Business*. Liesl, that beautiful Gargoyle, is lecturing Dunny Ramsay about the stupidity of his Calvinistic background. "But even Calvinism can be endured," she says, "if you will make some compromise with yourself. But you—there is a whole great piece of your life that is unlived, denied, set aside. That is why at fifty you can't bear it any longer and fly all to pieces and pour out your heart to the first really intelligent woman you have met—me, that's to say—and get into a schoolboy yearning for a girl who is as far from you as if she lived on the moon. This is the *revenge of the unlived life*" (italics mine).

I am now quite sure that Liesl's last sentence, above, is my source for Ham Walmsley's words from my own book. I am also sure that the Lena/Ham relationship draws heavily on the Dunny/Liesl relationship. I have always loved that part of *Fifth Business*. I must have carried this construct and these words somewhere inside, and when Ham begins his furtive ruminations on love and the desolation of his own life—there they were, these words. This concise wisdom. The writer in me chose them. A few years later, the author in me was embarrassed by them.

This distinction between writer and author is an important one, and perhaps more important now than ever before, because never before in literary history has the split between author and writer been wider. The writer is still the person who sits in a musty little room and scribbles things down. He's a dull fellow or gal but s/he does the real work of writing. The author is the one who *has written* it. He wears the ascot or she dresses all in black and signs copies of her books, says provocative things at readings, and lives in the world we call society. She is a public perception of the writer, sometimes even a public icon. She is just as often a fake, or he a dandy, a self-important bohemian who sits in cafés and flirts with waitresses and bemoans his state of misunderstood genius to all who will listen. Authors hold court. Only when they hold a pen are they writers once again.

When Chaucer translated the poets of the Italian Renaissance and borrowed from Boccaccio to write *Troilus and Criseyde*, it was the writer who did it. And thank God he did. Who would argue that Chaucer's poem about Troy isn't also a very English poem? When Shakespeare absorbed all those materials by Geoffrey of Monmouth, John Higgins, Edmund Spenser, and others for *King Lear*, again, the writer in him did it. To worry about literary lifting at the time of composition—to the writer then or now—would amount to so much fussiness. Such worries would interfere with the delicate process of a story or a poem unfolding. Such worries might well have inhibited the flowering of the English Renaissance. (Let us remember that Shakespeare *the author* has all but vanished from sight. We don't know who the hell he was. The more we speculate about it, the more we become suspect as scholars. Shakespeare the *writer*, now there's another case entirely.)

When it comes to the work of contemporary writers, I sometimes detect a bad smell hovering over conversations about the ways in which writers deploy their reading for their own purposes. How many times have I heard the phrase, that so and so's work *is too derivative*. Perhaps so and so's work *is* too derivative, but sometimes I can't escape the pervasive assumption that influence is a problem rather than a normal state of affairs. This assumption has evolved slowly over the last four centuries.

Thomas Mallon, the American English scholar and critic, gives a lively account of the evolution of literary borrowing of all kinds in his book *Stolen Words* (1989). He begins with the Aristotelian notion of literature born of imitation. Imitative writing was seen as a virtue. "The great critical cry of classical literature was not an Emersonian call to 'trust thyself' but a Horatian exhortation to follow others." Around the time of Shakespeare's rise in the theatre world, however, the virtues of imitation must have been wearing a bit thin. Elizabethan writers such as Robert Greene grumbled about Shakespeare's habit of borrowing plots. As writers began more and more to live by their pens instead of through the good graces of their patrons, they began to do more than grumble about borrowing. They began to make some unmistakably territorial sounds. Robert Burton (whose *Anatomy of Melancholy* [1621] was to be looted by Laurence Sterne) emerged to set the standard for acknowledged borrowing in the early seventeenth century. Mallon tells us that at this time "the word was getting around that words could be owned by their first writers" because literary property was now being thought of as "both imaginative and financial capital." We can trace this emerging attitude towards literary property by looking at the evolution of the word "plagiarism." In classical times, a "plagiary" (from the Latin *plagium*) was a kidnapper. Not until Ben Jonson readapted the term was it associated with literary theft. And it wasn't until the eighteenth century that we had an authoritative (albeit spare) definition of plagiarism, Samuel Johnson's: "Theft; literary adoption of the thoughts or works of another." This definition came about (mid-eighteenth century) when the notion of originality was beginning to spread. What oft was thought but ne'er so well expressed—the words themselves—had at last become a commodity. The fear in the mind of a seventeenth century writer, that he might be vilified as a word-for-word plagiarist, became an official crime in the eighteenth century. In the nineteenth century, again in England, originality had finally become an orthodoxy, and the copyright statute was amended so that a writer's publication was protected for forty-two years after publication. If plagiarism and copyright piracy in the England of Dickens was still a concern, in America it was a veritable plague. Not until the end of the nineteenth century did Americans begin to honour the spirit of English copyright laws. Mallon tells us that "only in 1988 did the Senate vote to allow American participation in the Berne Convention on international copyright that was drawn up in 1886." The world and all of literature has always been the storehouse of the writer. But what is storehouse to the writer is now a loans department to the author.

It's fair to assume that with the growth of our notions about originality and literary theft came a more intense awareness of shame and infamy at being accused of plagiarism. Indeed, for most authors surveyed in Mallon's book, the greatest fear was not of lawsuits but of the moral stigma of getting caught in a furtive act: using the materials and especially the words of other writers without proper acknowledgement. The more readers and writers revered "originality" as an absolute artistic virtue, the more the spectre of guilt floated over the "influenced" writer's horizon.

The influenced writer. Does that sound like a euphemism? Alert readers of the world, merlin-eyed scholars: I beg you to think otherwise.

Even with the proliferation of electronic technology, the world of the writer hasn't changed much. Writers are still at their best alone with a story in a private little room. But the world of the author has changed drastically. Authors must learn how to project a public image. To sell their books, they must become *good copy.* It helps if they look good on television. Once they have become well enough known to make a living by their words, they need good agents and lawyers. Now that film and television contracts constitute a large chunk of the successful author's income, the money stakes are much higher. The author is more like a sports hero or a corporate star than ever before, and since authors live very much in the world, their ethics must conform even more to the rules of corporate law. As businessmen and women they are disengaged from the thing they do best: pecking away in their studies or garrets, where imagination is the only legislator, and where conscience has more to do with getting it right than trying not to offend other writers. Little wonder that dullard pecking away in the garret is so much happier. The writer can forget for a little while that he or she is compelled to be an author.

When my brother and I were small boys, in wintertime we would play on the living room floor with our box of metal cowboys and Indians, engaging them in a perpetual battle that rang throughout the house. On certain days my mother would come along to hoover the floor. In our house, one did not vacuum; one hoovered. We had scarcely acquired this machine when it became a verb.

"Out of my way, you varmints," she would say. "When I'm hoovering rugs, nothing escapes this machine."

The hoover sucked up dirt, nails, toys, lint, fuzzy candies, and coins with an impressive lack of discrimination. With a little imagination, our hoover could become a science fiction nightmare. Sometimes my brother, being an older brother, would object to this invasion.

My mother's reply was usually something like this: "You can do without cowboys and Indians for a few minutes, but you can't do without a clean house. Vamoose!"

Thus the birth of authoritarian morality.

David Williams, wherever you are, I was hoovering for art's sake. At the very first time of composition at Fort San, Saskatchewan, I may have been aware that the phrase "the revenge of the unlived life" had come from the pen of Robertson Davies. The more I think about it, my character Lena Rotzoll from "Jokes" shares a great deal with Liesl. I may have been aware that I was using a phrase from Davies's book but, if I was, I brushed this awareness aside, because in the fever of composing a first draft, these were the right words. In the subsequent drafts I paid no attention to these words—unless it was to congratulate myself on them.

Some readers might well wonder if there is any such thing as plagiarism. I believe there is. If I copy down someone else's words or ideas and pass them off holus-bolus as my own, I am plagiarizing. If I copy down someone else's poem—even if I've just translated it—and say to my reading audience, "See how clever and wise and sensitive I am," I am a plagiarist plain and simple. Again, Thomas Mallon is helpful here. The writer, he claims, "need not blush about stealing if he makes what he takes completely his, if he alchemizes it into something that is . . . thoroughly new." But this form of enlightened lifting "is not put unchanged onto the dinner table by someone who pretends he's been cooking all day."

How much is too much? To make judgements on this question the literary sleuth looks for an entire pattern of stolen words and ideas done with unmistakable cunning. But hoovering up a plot (or an idea, a maxim, a character, a technique, a moral dilemma, a phrase) for one's own use is as common for the writer as breathing. Tracing the process of lifting or any other legitimate kind of influence leads us into labyrinths as byzantine as the human mind. At best this is a fascinating exercise in the impossible. But this much I can say with a degree of certainty. Murdoch lifts from Herodotus enough so that her own characters can become modern, ironic reflections of the original story. Davies tries Herodotus on for size and Murdoch too. He isn't drawn much to Murdoch's comedy of manners where intelligent characters seethe with futility, but he seems to love Honor Klein every bit as much as I love Liesl. John Irving leaves Herodotus alone, and demonstrates little patience with Davies's many monologues and his bowing towards the superior wisdom of Europe, but he seems drawn to Davies's full rendering of grotesques, his intellectual vigour, and his skill in recounting a spiritual journey full of miracles. Murdoch, and then Davies, make fascinating use of heads without torsos. Irving leaves the head and arms, and takes the torso.

The supreme lifter would seem to be Davies. His debt to Iris Murdoch probably goes beyond what my summary has revealed, but he has written such a fascinating novel, such an *original* novel, that he easily escapes my earliest suspicions of excessive borrowing. In fact, *Fifth Business* is a livelier novel than *A Severed Head*. For all its wit and sophistication, Murdoch's early novel never gets out of the drawing room and into the dark gods, the *ékstasis* of Martin's awakening. But Davies's novel not only promises a world of wonders for his improbable grump of a hero; he delivers on these wonders.

I have a writer's memory, not a scholar's. Perhaps I have very little to teach the scholars who make their living from close and careful reading. Perhaps only this: that when the words or ideas of another writer find their way unacknowledged into a lively and original tale, well, sometimes a good hoover doesn't discriminate too well when it's sucking things up. It is too busy going about its work. It just moves forward in a fine frenzy rolling. It has been doing this from before Genesis 1:1. And sometimes still, it does this in a sacred cause.